MINI WEAPONS
OF MASS DESTRUCTION

**MAKE MAYHEM FROM YOUR STATIONERY
WITH 35 MODELS TO BUILD YOURSELF**

JOHN AUSTIN

ilex

To all those brave little green army men who experienced horrible melting deaths and are now buried in millions of unmarked sandbox graves. And of course to my father, Steve Austin, who bought me all those courageous PVC soldiers.

An Hachette UK Company
www.hachette.co.uk

First published in Great Britain in 2017 by Ilex, a division of Octopus Publishing Group Ltd
Carmelite House
50 Victoria Embankment
London EC4Y 0DZ
www.octopusbooks.co.uk

Originally published by Chicago Review Press, Incorporated
814 North Franklin Street
Chicago, Illinois 60610

Publisher: Roly Allen
Editorial Director: Zara Larcombe
Commissioning Editor: Zara Anvari
Managing Specialist Editor: Frank Gallaugher
Editor: Francesca Leung
Admin Assistant: Sarah Vaughan
Art Director: Julie Weir
Artworker: Ginny Zeal
Production Controller: Marina Maher

ISBN 978-1-78157-499-7

A CIP catalogue record for this book is available from the British Library.

Printed and bound in the UK
10 9 8 7 6 5 4 3 2

This book contains a variety of projects to transform everyday objects into small weapons, including projectiles and explosives. Projectiles can be fired forcefully and can cause damage, and the explosives are loud and can cause damage, hearing impairment or hearing loss. Eye protection must be worn when experimenting with any of these projects and ear protection is recommended for all explosives. Neither Octopus Publishing Group Limited or the author take any responsibility for any injury or damage resulting from the use or misuse of information contained in this book.

>>>

CONTENTS

INTRODUCTION

MINI WEAPONS OF MASS DESTRUCTION is a humorous tactical guide that illustrates the potential of everyday items to be transformed into a menacing mini arsenal.

This bible of forbidden knowledge will prepare you for a zombie uprising or the inevitable alien invasion. To prevent mass hysteria, proper training is essential. Each weapon is catalogued with an easy-to-read bill of materials, step-by-step instructions and alternate construction methods. And in the final chapter you'll find a small library of simple targets you can use to master your Mini Weapon shooting skills.

This is a book for warriors of all ages. It pushes the laws of physics, inspires creativity, proposes experimentation and fuels the imagination. Many of the catapults and launchers are great representations of their real-life counterparts, but they cost only pennies, making them great for group exercises and perfect for large-quantity builds.

This book is for entertainment purposes only. Please review the safety page for your personal protection. Build and use these projects at your own risk.

>>>

PLAY IT SAFE

THE UNEXPECTED CAN ALWAYS HAPPEN! When building and firing Mini Weapons, be responsible and take every safety precaution. Switching materials, substituting ammunition, assembling improperly, mishandling, targeting inaccurately and misfiring can all cause harm. You should always be prepared for the unknown. *Eye protection is a must* if you chose to experiment with any of these projects.

Always be aware of your environment, including any spectators and flammable materials, and be careful when handling the launchers. Devices that are based on combustion shooters require gaseous fuel; always start with a small amount of the recommended aerosol, then gradually increase the amount to determine what you need for a successful launch. Crossbows and darts have dangerous points, and elastic and latex shooters fire projectiles at unbelievable force and can cause damage. Never point these launchers at people, animals or anything of value.

It is important to remember that since mini weaponry is homebuilt, it is not always accurate. Basic target blueprints are available at the back of the book; use these to test the accuracy of your Mini Weapons.

This book also features mini bombs. Despite their names, they could never be modified to do serious damage. However, they are very loud and can cause hearing impairment or even hearing loss. *Ear protection is recommended* for all bombs.

Always be responsible when constructing and using mini weaponry. It is important that you understand that the author, the publisher and the bookseller cannot and will not guarantee your safety. When you try the projects described here, you do so at your own risk. They are *not* toys!

1

SMALL
LAUNCHERS

BB PENCIL

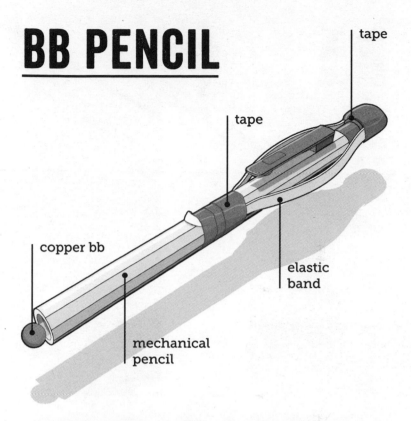

tape

tape

copper bb

elastic
band

mechanical
pencil

The BB Pencil is a small, pocket-sized rifle designed to launch a single BB elastically. Requiring limited supplies, this is a great mechanical gun with incredible accuracy. The pencil retains its original form, making it easy to conceal in plain sight – the perfect double-agent tool.

SUPPLIES	TOOLS	AMMO
1 inexpensive mechanical pencil	Safety Glasses	10+ BBs
1 wide elastic band	Scissors (or craft knife)	
Masking or duct tape		

RANGE
6–9m

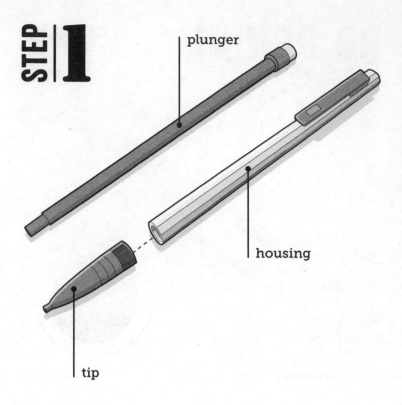

plunger

housing

tip

Dissect your inexpensive mechanical pencil using brute strength. Pull out the innards and snap off the pencil tip. If you are unable to perform the decapitation by hand, use pliers. Once removed, the pencil tip can be discarded.

The outer housing of the pencil becomes the barrel of the BB Pencil. Make sure the housing pathway is unobstructed by any plastic fragments that might have broken off while disassembling the pencil.

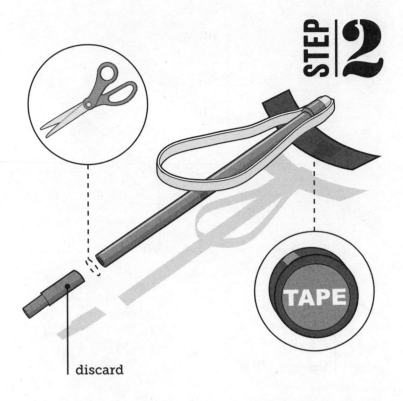

discard

TAPE

Carefully use scissors or a craft knife to remove the tapered end of the plunger. This will make room for the BB to sit in the barrel, waiting to be launched, and prevent it from falling out.

Next, securely fasten a wide elastic band to the rubber end of the plunger with tape. If the rubber is newer, cut a slit in the rubber to slide the elastic band into for additional support.

STEP | 3

Once you have modified the plunger, slide it back into the pencil housing barrel.

Lay the elastic band on top of the pencil housing. Eliminate any slack in the elastic band and securely fasten it to the pencil housing with tape. Any malfunction during operation will be directly related to the taping of the elastic band, so make sure it's secure.

Your BB Pencil is now fully operational. Load a single BB into the muzzle end of the barrel and choose your target carefully. Then pull back the plunger and let it rip!

This mechanical marvel is capable of firing BBs with incredible force and can cause damage. It is important to remember this Mini Weapon is homebuilt and not always accurate. If you wish to test your BB Pencil, basic targets are available in chapter 7.

ALTERNATE CONSTRUCTION

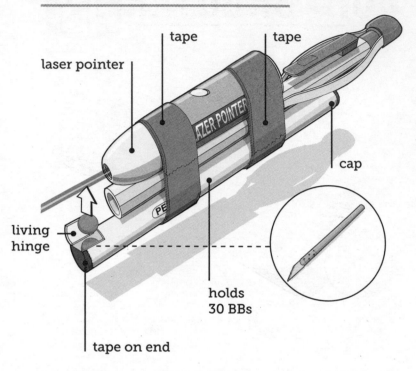

tape

tape

laser pointer

cap

living hinge

holds 30 BBs

tape on end

With a few simple additions, you can modify your BB Pencil by incorporating an advanced laser targeting system with additional ammo rounds at your fingertips.

Using an emptied-out pen housing, cut a small BB-sized door at the open end. Then use a small piece of tape to cap the open end. The housing should hold about 30 BBs and can easily be dumped out for a quick reload.

Next, tape both the pen housing and a small, inexpensive laser pointer onto your BB Pencil. Turn on your pointer when you are ready to fire.

COIN SHOOTER

balloon

toilet roll tube

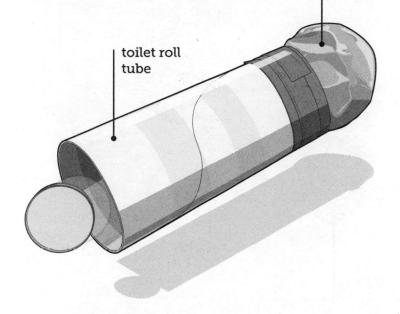

Everyone on the ground – the party's over! The Coin Shooter is an amazing, inexpensive elastic launcher with an incredible range. Because the gun housing is made from a recycled toilet roll tube and a balloon, you'll not only be firing pennies, you'll also be saving them.

SUPPLIES
1 balloon
1 toilet roll tube
Duct tape

TOOLS
Safety Glasses
Scissors

AMMO
1+ coins

RANGE
3–18m

>>>

STEP 1

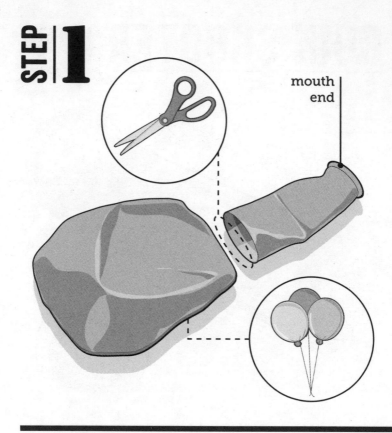

mouth end

Using scissors, cut one standard-sized latex balloon in half as shown. Throw the mouth end away or recycle it; you will not need it for this build.

Now it's time to manufacture the barrel of your elastic cannon. Toilet roll tubes are ideal for this component. If toilet rolls are not available, you can find thick, sturdy tubes inside rolls of paper towels, aluminium foil and wrapping paper.

Pull the balloon head that you cut over the end of the cardboard cylinder. Once in place, tape it securely into position without denting or crushing the tube. Then once taped, pull the balloon back to test your adhesive restraint. Add more tape if needed. It is important that you do not alter the tube diameter when securing the tape. This will affect the efficiency of the launcher.

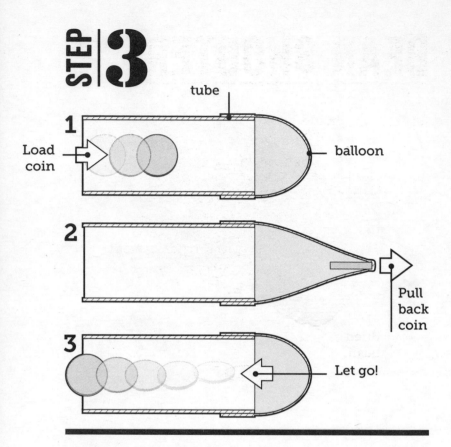

tube

1 Load coin

balloon

2 Pull back coin

3 Let go!

Now load a coin into the muzzle end of the shooter. With your fingers, locate the ammunition in the balloon. Holding the coin between your fingers, pull back the balloon and safely aim the muzzle away from spectators and anything breakable. Release your ammunition from your grip and let it go! The latex will catapult your coin through the barrel at high velocity.

Replacing the short barrel with a longer barrel will help with the accuracy of this firearm. Also, although the gun is designed to launch coins, other low-cost ammunition can be used instead – rubbers, marshmallows, paper clips, pen caps, small foldback clips, peanuts, bouncy balls and small sweets.

Never operate the launcher if the balloon is starting to show signs of wear.

BEAN SHOOTER

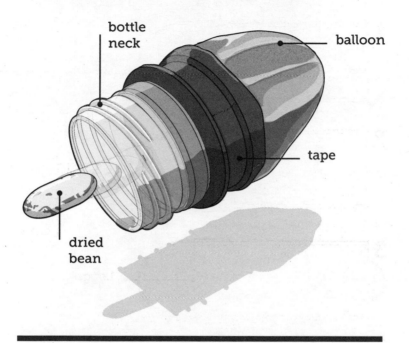

bottle neck

balloon

tape

dried bean

The Bean Shooter is the perfect pocket-sized latex launcher. With its unbreakable plastic frame design and commanding firepower, it's ideal for the on-the-go hobbyist sharpshooter.

SUPPLIES

1 plastic bottle
1 balloon
Duct tape

TOOLS

Safety glasses
Penknife
Scissors

AMMO

1+ dried beans

RANGE

3–18m

>>>

STEP 1

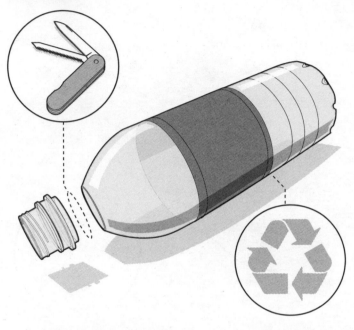

With over 20 billion bottles of water sold each year, finding a suitable Bean Shooter frame shouldn't be a problem. How about recycling one of those billons into a musket marvel?

Using one of your penknife blades, cut off the threaded neck of a plastic bottle. Once you have removed the neck, use your knife to trim off any sharp protrusions that may be left on the cut edge.

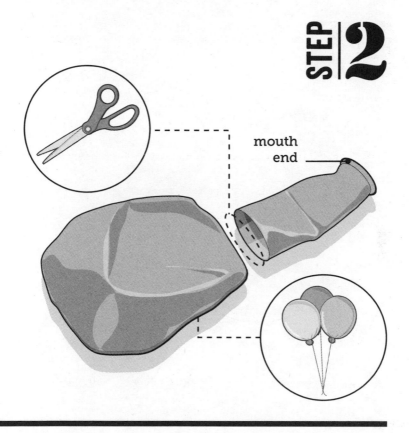

mouth end

Like the Coin Shooter, the Bean Shooter's power source is a standard-sized latex balloon. Using scissors, cut the balloon in half as shown and discard the mouth end.

Balloons come in many shapes and sizes. A traditional round balloon is recommended for this type of launcher, but feel free to test other balloon shapes for varied results.

STEP 3

TAPE

Assembly of your Bean Shooter is quick and easy. Take the half section of the balloon and tape it tightly to the bottle top. It is important to be certain that you've cleaned up the cut edge of the bottle as described in step 1. Sharp edges will cut your balloon and cause a malfunction.

Now, load a dried bean, rubber or peanut into the barrel and locate it with your fingers. Once you have a grip on it, pull it back and release. It is important that you pick a safe target on which to practise your marksmanship.

CLOTHES PEG SHOOTER

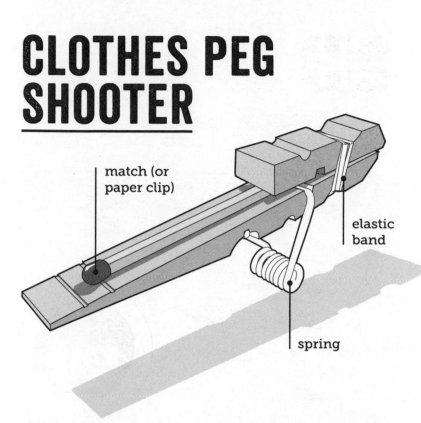

match (or paper clip)

elastic band

spring

Yes, people still use wooden clothes pegs. You'll be using one to construct a menacing spear gun capable of firing flaming matches. Held like a gun and fired like a gun, this Mini Weapon will have wrongdoers reaching for the sky.

SUPPLIES

1 wooden clothes peg
1 elastic band

TOOLS

Safety glasses
Penknife

AMMO

1+ wooden matches
or paper clips

RANGE

3m

STEP 1

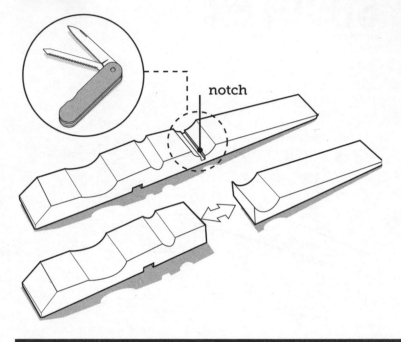

notch

First, disassemble a clothes peg and lay the two wooden prongs and metal spring on a cutting surface.

Use one of the blades of a penknife to modify the two halves. First, cut a small notch into one of the wooden prongs, as shown. Take your time! Fingers cost more than clothes pegs. Then, cut the other prong in half at the location shown in the above illustration.

STEP 2

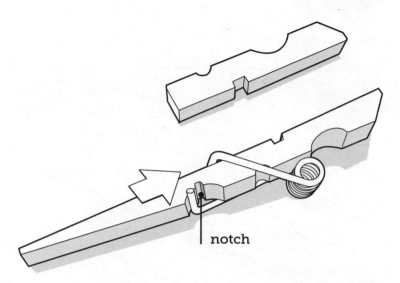

notch

Tightly slide the factory spring back onto the prong with the custom notch you cut out in step 1. Use the illustration above to make sure the spring is properly oriented. Continue to slide the spring until the bar snaps into the notch. If your notch does not seem deep enough, rework it.

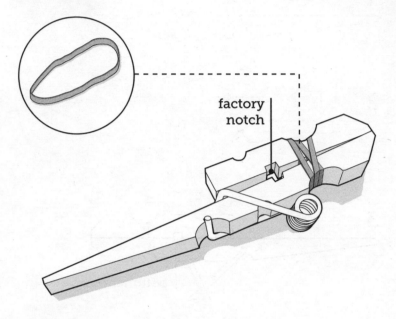

factory notch

Next, place the shorter wooden prong on top of the longer section. Use the factory notches as a point of reference before sandwiching the two prongs together. Once in place, secure the halves with an elastic band.

Wrap the elastic band just tight enough that you can still move the prongs. To get an idea of how much they should move, keep in mind that the top prong will ultimately slide forward to cock the spring into place.

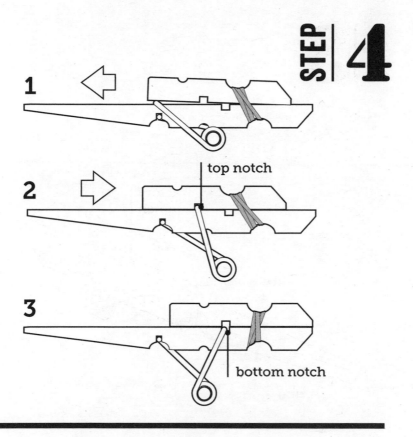

1

top notch

2

3

bottom notch

Now it's time to lock and load your clothes peg launcher for its first test fire. Push the top prong forwards until the spring arm is caught in the top factory notch. Once it is in place, slowly slide the prong back until the spring arm snaps into the bottom notch on the lower prong.

STEP 5

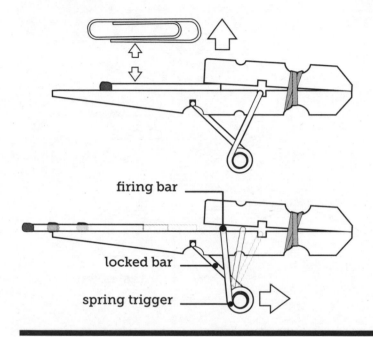

firing bar

locked bar

spring trigger

'Hands in the air!' Load your projectile into the launcher by lifting the top prong. Wooden matches or standard paper clips are recommended for best results.

Once loaded, pull back the spring trigger to release the firing bar. If the launcher does not fire, but the spring arm in the locked bar pops out, make the locked bar notch deeper. Malfunctions commonly occur if the notch is too shallow.

You can stick a matchbox striking pad to the prong barrel to light the match when it launches, giving a flaming arrow. (For a strike-anywhere match, a small piece of sandpaper can be used instead of the striking pad.) For this modification, it is best to reverse the match head, or a simpler solution is to light the match before firing. Flaming ammunition is not recommended for indoor use. Remove all flammable materials from the area and always wear safety glasses.

PEG SHOOTER

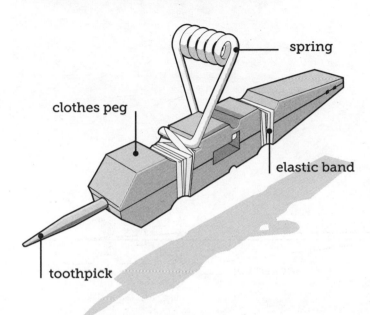

spring

clothes peg

elastic band

toothpick

This miniature, spring-powered Peg Shooter is ideal for launching a hailstorm of toothpick firepower. With its palm-sized proportions and quick reload, this shooter is designed for one honourable goal: hanging the laundry out to dry.

SUPPLIES
1 wooden clothes peg
2 elastic bands

TOOLS
Safety glasses
Penknife

AMMO
1+ toothpicks

RANGE
3m

STEP 1

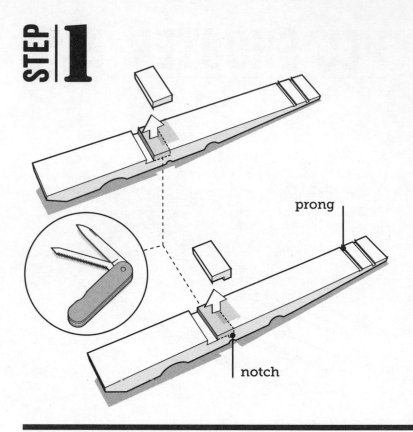

prong

notch

Disassemble a clothes peg so that you have two wooden prongs and a small metal spring.

You are going to make similar notches in both prongs. However, the notch in one prong will be slightly different from the other prong with a larger notched area. Examine the two illustrations carefully to see the difference. Take your time cutting the notches – craftsmanship is key.

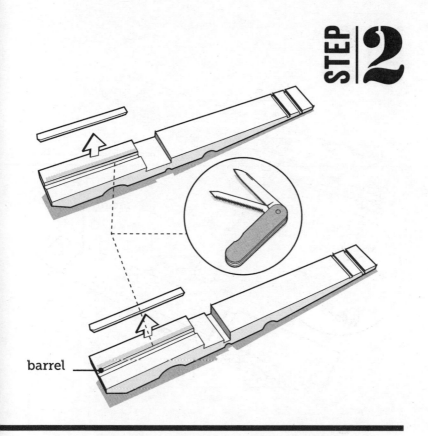

barrel

Using a penknife, carve a small groove into each prong using a blade that you feel comfortable with. Remember to be careful when handling the blade. Once the prongs are sandwiched together, the grooves should create a channel that is slightly larger than the diameter of a toothpick. This channel will become the Peg Shooter's barrel.

A straight barrel always helps with the accuracy of any gun, so it may help to draw your cut lines on the prongs using a ruler as a guide.

STEP 3

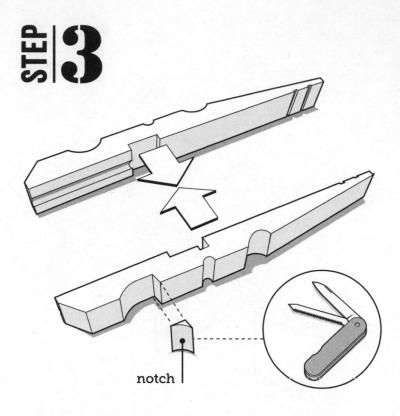

notch

Before sandwiching the prongs together back to back, you will need to remove more material. On the lower prong, at one end of the factory curve, slice the wood to create a 90-degree angle on the curve's back wall, as shown.

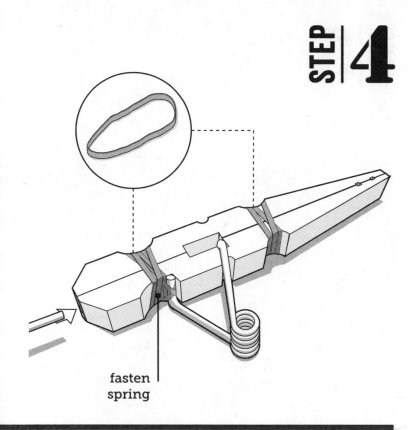

fasten
spring

Now it's time to assemble the Peg Shooter. Hold the two prongs with the flat sides pressed together. Once the prongs are aligned, wrap an elastic band around each set of factory curves, at the front and back of the wooden gun. Fine string can also be substituted. Do not obstruct the centre of the prongs; this area is reserved for the spring assembly.

Next, wedge the clothes peg spring into the wood assembly as shown. One spring arm should be wedged beneath the front elastic band support. (Fastening the front spring underneath the elastic band will help manage its position.) The other spring arm should be inserted in the middle notch.

STEP | 5

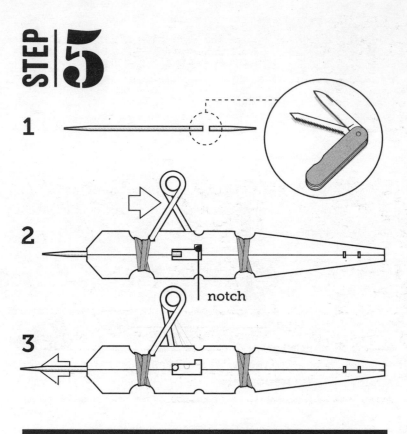

1

2

notch

3

First prepare the arrow. Take a standard round toothpick and cut off one point. This modified toothpick is your ammo.

Now to lock and load your Peg Shooter. Cock the spring back into its custom notch. Cocking the spring may be tricky and will require one hand to hold the peg gun while the other negotiates the spring into its locked position. Slide the blunt end of the modified toothpick into the muzzle end of the barrel. Point your Shooter safely at a target and, using your finger, pull back the spring so it releases and propels the toothpick forwards. If the toothpick doesn't fire, check your spring to see if the notch is too big. If this is the case, you will have to make a new modified wooden prong with a smaller notch.

Remember: safety first. You are shooting a fine-tipped arrow out of a homemade launcher. Always wear safety glasses and never point the Peg Shooter at anyone.

TUBE LAUNCHER

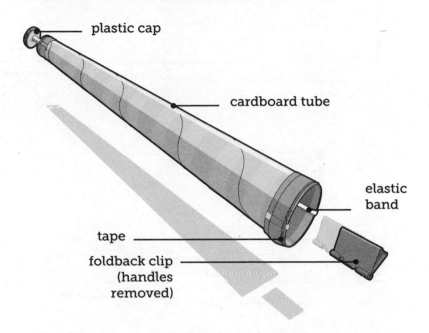

plastic cap

cardboard tube

elastic band

tape

foldback clip (handles removed)

The Tube Launcher is also known as the Rock Launcher. Its universal design makes it a great launcher for almost any ammunition.

SUPPLIES
1 cork
1 paper clip
Duct tape
2 wide elastic bands
Cardboard tube
String
2 plastic caps
  (from plastic
  milk bottles)

TOOLS
Safety glasses
Scissors
Penknife

AMMO
1+ small foldback
  clips (19 mm),
  handles removed
  (see page 40 on
  how to remove)

RANGE
6m

>>>

STEP 1

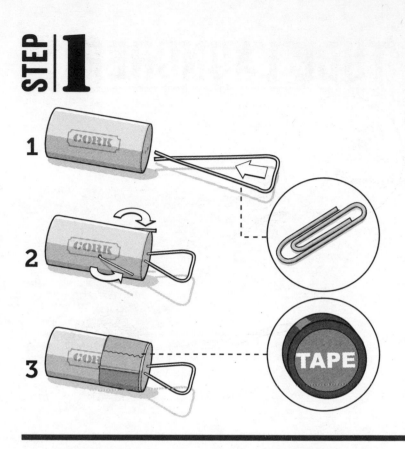

First, select a cork that fits easily inside your cardboard tube. You want to have some clearance on the walls, because you will be adding additional diameter to the cork.

Straighten a paper clip and then bend it into a U shape as shown in illustration #1, above. Next, slowly push both ends of the paper clip into the cork. Aim the ends of the paper clip so that they poke out of the sides of the cork around its midpoint. Bend the ends upwards (illustration #2, above) to prevent the paper clip from coming out.

Finally, use tape to wrap up the ends of the paper clip so they do not scrape against the inside of the tube. Test your cork by sliding it through the tube before proceeding to the next step. Rework the paper clip's positioning if the cork jams in the tube.

Now it's time to add the elastic firepower to this Tube Launcher. Using scissors, cut both elastic bands to give two pieces of elastic that are equal in length. Tape the elastic band pieces to the end of the cork opposite the paper clip. When taping the bands it is important to leave their ends sticking out a bit so you can fold them back and tape them a second time. This will help prevent the elastic bands from stretching out of their tape restraints. This is one area that is prone to malfunction, so do a thorough taping job here. For additional holding power, use heavy-duty staples.

STEP | 3

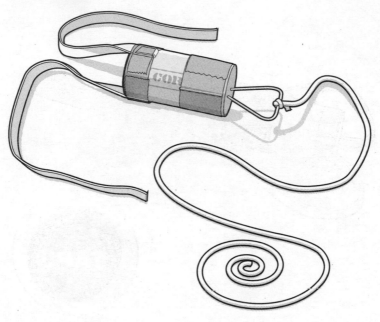

Cut a piece of string that is longer than the length of the card-board tube. Tie one end of the string to the paper clip. This string will be subjected to tremendous force when you use the Tube Launcher, so it is important that it has some pulling strength. Double-check your knot. You don't want it to give way while the cork is in the tube. Disassembling the launcher at that point would be annoying... so triple check it.

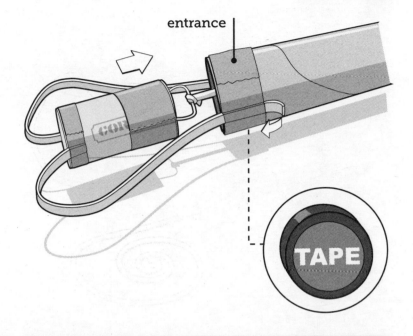

entrance

TAPE

Now it's time to install the components into the cardboard tube. Slide the string and cork assembly into the tube – string and paper clip first. Tape both ends of the elastic bands parallel to each other on the outside of the tube, as shown. Then fold the elastic bands back towards themselves and put more tape over them. These areas also experience tremendous pressure, so it is important to tape them well to avoid malfunction.

STEP 5

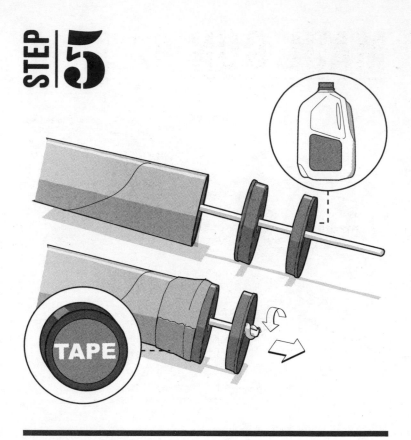

TAPE

Now that the entrance assembly is finished, it's time to work on the other end.

First, locate two large plastic milk bottle caps. Using a pen-knife, cut a small hole in the centre of each. Mirroring one another, back-to-back, run the string through the centre of the caps. Fasten the cap closest to the tube with tape.

Now, slowly pull the string until you feel some tension from the elastic bands. Tie a few knots at the end so that the string can't pass through the hole in the cap. Depending on the size of the hole, you may want to add a large paper clip to the end of the string as well.

Load your ammunition and pull back on the outermost bottle cap. Release the cap and watch your ammo fly!

MAUL GUN

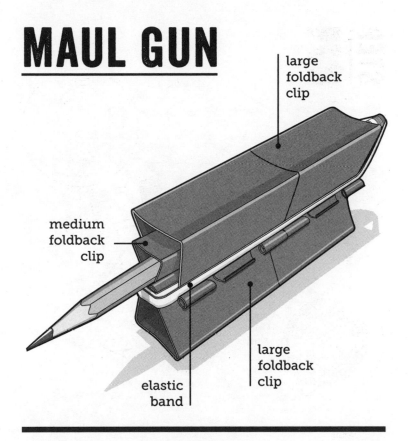

large
foldback
clip

medium
foldback
clip

large
foldback
clip

elastic
band

The Maul Gun's raw power can pierce an aluminium can with
ease. But because it's so powerful, it is also dangerous and
should be operated with care. It is not very accurate because of
the somewhat random directions its pencil exits the barrel, but
is great for short-distance accuracy tests or long-distance
range contests. Never place your intended target in front of
breakable materials such as glass, thin wood or ceramic.

SUPPLIES

3 medium foldback
  clips (32 mm)
4 large foldback
  clips (51 mm)
2 wide elastic bands

TOOLS

Safety glasses

AMMO

1 pencil

RANGE
6–9m

STEP 1

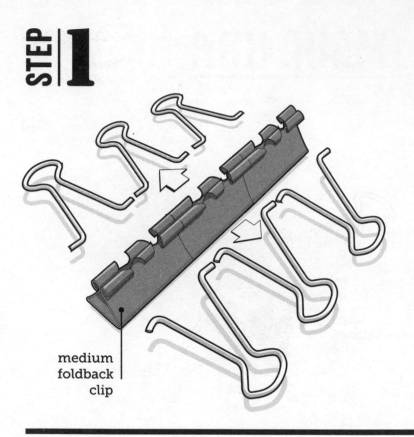

medium
foldback
clip

Remove the metal handles from three medium foldback clips (32 mm) by squeezing the handles from the sides, then pulling them out. These metal handles can be discarded or recycled, for they are not used in the Maul Gun. Arrange the three foldback clips in a line, facing upwards.

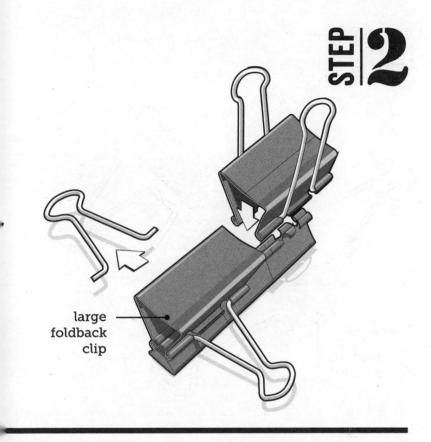

large
foldback
clip

Next, clip two large foldback clips (51 mm) onto the row of medium foldback clips. Once hooked, the assembly should be completely attached so you can easily lift it as one piece.

Remove the metal handles from the large foldback clips only after you've clipped them securely in place.

STEP | 3

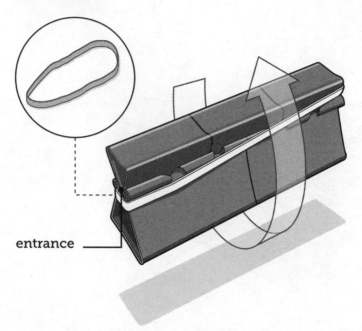

entrance

Rotate the assembly so that the medium foldback clips are now on top. Loop one end of a wide and durable elastic band onto the assembly so it does not obstruct your entrance; the other end of the elastic band should cover the medium fold-back hole in the rear.

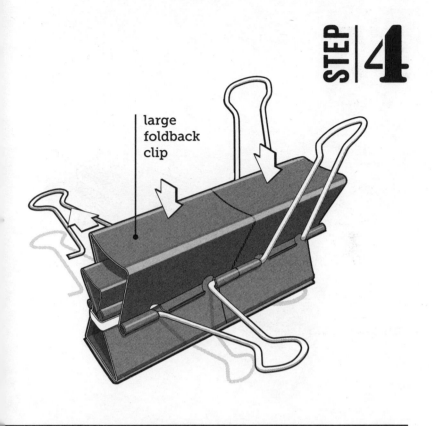

large
foldback
clip

Next, clip two more large foldback clips (51 mm) onto the row of medium foldback clips, as shown. Once clamped on, the large foldback clips should hold the elastic band in place.

Remove the metal handles from the large foldback clips after you've secured them in place.

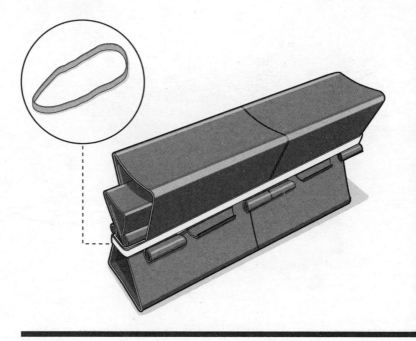

Place an additional wide elastic band around the newly placed large foldback clips. This will add some additional support for the Maul Gun and prevent the foldback clips from sliding off.

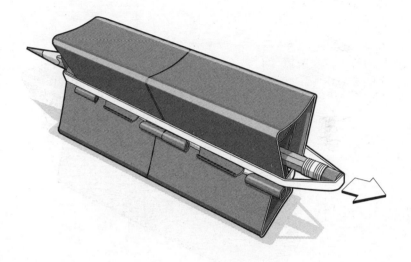

Time to fire the Maul Gun! Load a pencil or pen into the muzzle end (entrance) of the barrel. Pull the pencil and elastic band back, and once you've determined a safe target, release the elastic band.

Unsharpened pencils, markers, highlighters and capped pens can all be used for ammo. A sharpened pencil is not necessary unless you are hunting aluminium cans. For safe target suggestions, visit chapter 7.

ALTERNATE CONSTRUCTION

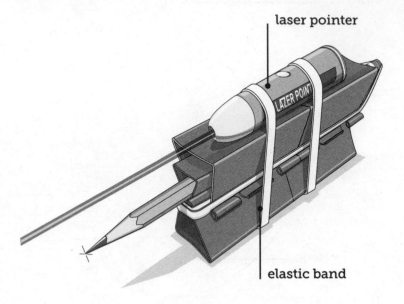

laser pointer

elastic band

To help with accuracy and control of your Maul Gun, mount a laser pointer on top of the foldback clips using elastic bands. Sight in a few times and adjust the trajectory of the red dot. This upgrade should help you narrow in on your next non-living target.

AIR VORTEX

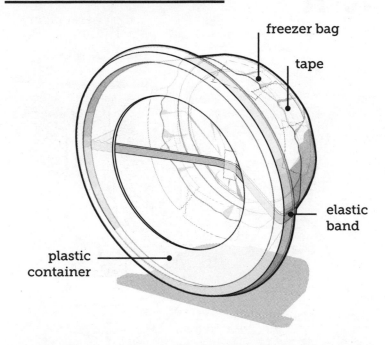

freezer bag

tape

elastic band

plastic container

With limited damaging powers, the Air Vortex probably can't take on much more than shattering a few helpless card houses. However, this project has huge potential for varied uses, such as extinguishing a candle, blowing smoke or creating smoke rings. Explore these possibilities by performing experiments with containers of different widths and depths.

SUPPLIES

1 circular plastic
    container with lid
1 freezer bag
1 wide elastic band
Transparent or
    packing tape

TOOLS

1 drinking glass
1 marker
1 craft knife
1 small plate

AMMO

Air

RANGE

60–150cm

>>>

STEP 1

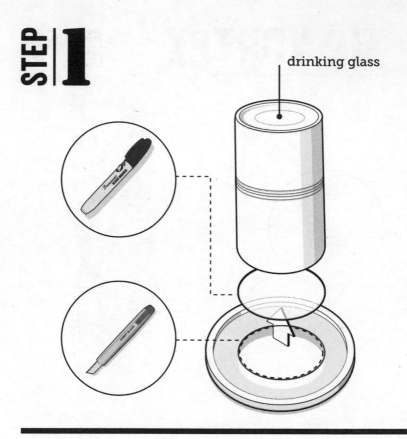

drinking glass

Use the drinking glass and marker to trace a circle in the centre of the container lid. The area to be removed should be a few centimetres smaller than the diameter of the container. Then use a craft knife to cut the marked circle out of the lid.

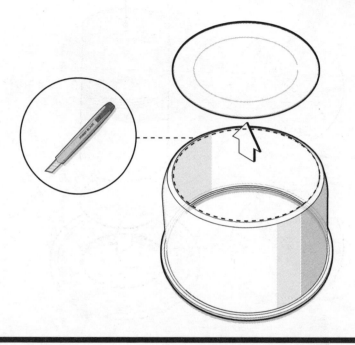

Now flip the plastic container upside down so that the bottom is facing upwards. Use your craft knife to safely cut out the bottom around the outer edge. The plastic's thickness will affect how easy it is to remove, so be careful and take your time. You will not be using the removed container bottom, so you may recycle it.

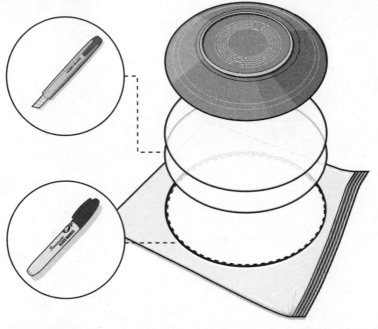

Now prepare the plastic freezer bag. Find a large freezer bag and a dinner plate for tracing. The plate's diameter should be a few centimetres larger than the diameter of the container you have chosen. If you have decided to build this vortex out of a larger container or cardboard box, a plastic bag or bin liner can also be used.

Place the plate upside down on the freezer bag and trace around it with a marker. Then use scissors or a craft knife to cut out the circle. You will need only one of the plastic circles for this project. Discard the remaining scrap.

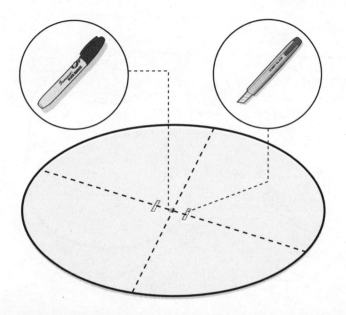

To determine the centre point of the plastic circle, fold it in half, and then fold it again. Unfold the circle and use your marker to place a small dot on the point where the two folds intersect – this is the centre point.

Using a craft knife, cut two small slits into the plastic, as shown. These slits will ultimately hold the wide elastic band, and so should be roughly the same size as the width of the wide elastic band – don't make the slits too large.

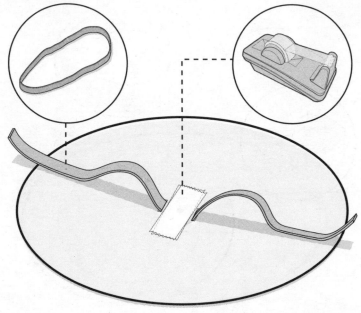

Use scissors to cut the wide elastic band. Slide the band through the slits in the plastic circle. Once you've centred the elastic band, add tape to the area between the slits to increase its strength. This added support should help prevent tearing during use.

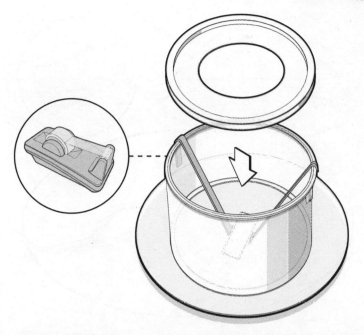

Now place the container, right side up, on top of the plastic circle, as shown above. Pull the two ends of the elastic band over the rim of the container, parallel to each another. Tape the ends securely to the outside of the container.

Next, snap on the modified container cover. Once it is on, the cover should help hold the elastic band in place. But if the cover isn't holding, add more tape.

STEP 7

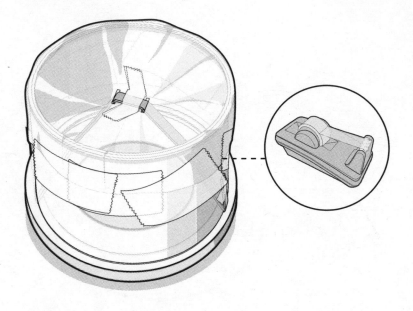

Turn the plastic container over and bend the freezer bag over the sidewalls. Once the plastic is in place, go tape-crazy. When you are finished, the bond should be airtight.

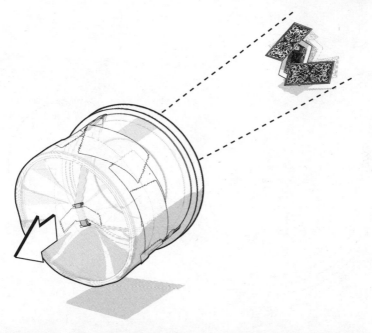

Time to destroy something! Pull back the area where the elastic band and plastic meet in the back, then release. The Air Vortex will release a gust of air directed at your target.

This is a great project that encourages experimentation. Containers of different sizes, including boxes and cardboard cylindrical snack tubes, will produce varying results. This makes for the perfect inexpensive assignment for a group of individuals battling it out with science and physics.

The Air Vortex is completely harmless, but use the craft knife with care.

2

BOWS AND SLINGSHOTS

SIMPLE CROSSBOW

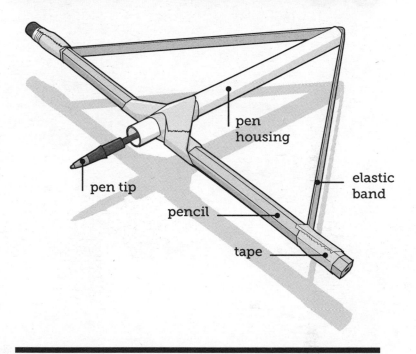

pen housing

pen tip

elastic band

pencil

tape

Simple is right! This basic pistol crossbow can be assembled in seconds. Its small size and minimal parts list make it a great introductory bow. The elastic band, mounted on top of the pen housing stock, makes firing ink bolts easy and quick.

SUPPLIES

1 unsharpened pencil
Masking or duct tape (duct tape works best)
1 wide elastic band

TOOLS

Safety glasses
Penknife or pliers (optional)
Scissors

AMMO

1 pen

RANGE

3–9m

STEP 1

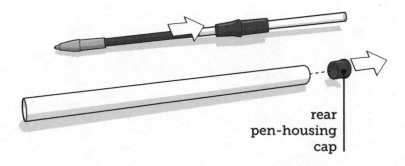

rear
pen-housing
cap

Dismantle a plastic ballpoint pen into its parts. Depending on how the pen has been manufactured, you may need a tool to assist you with dislodging the rear pen-housing cap. A pen-knife (for cutting it off) or small pliers (for pulling it out) can both work well. Once the pen has been taken apart, make sure the ink cartridge can pass through the pen housing. If it can't, cut an inch off your pen housing. This will allow you to pull back your ink bolt before launch.

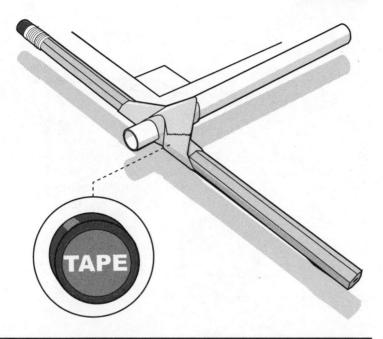

Place the hollowed-out pen housing over your unsharpened pencil as in the illustration above. Notice that it is centred on the pencil, but only a short part of the pen housing sticks out in front. Once the pencil and pen are correctly positioned, tape the pen in place. It may take some additional taping to help centre the pen housing. A 90-degree angle is ideal.

STEP 3

TAPE

Cut a wide elastic band using scissors. Tape the ends of the elastic band to the ends of the pencil as shown above. You may want to tie or wrap the elastic band around the ends of the pencil before taping it in place. This will increase the bond.

Now load your pen-ink bolt into the muzzle end of the housing. Pull both the elastic band and the pen tip backwards, then release. Because of the light weight of your arrow, accuracy will be limited. Always operate with safety glasses.

CLIP CROSSBOW

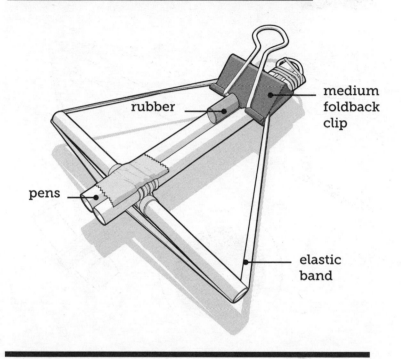

rubber

medium
foldback
clip

pens

elastic
band

The Clip Crossbow is a great universal Mini Weapon with endless ammo possibilities. It's designed to hold the bow in a fully drawn position until you are ready to release the foldback-clip trigger – just like a real crossbow! Once it's complete, you'll enjoy its single-hand operation.

SUPPLIES

3 pens
4 thin elastic bands
1 medium foldback
   clip (32 mm)
1 wide elastic band
Tape (any kind)

TOOLS

Safety glasses
Craft knife
Pliers (optional)

AMMO

1 rubber

RANGE

3–9m

>>>

STEP 1

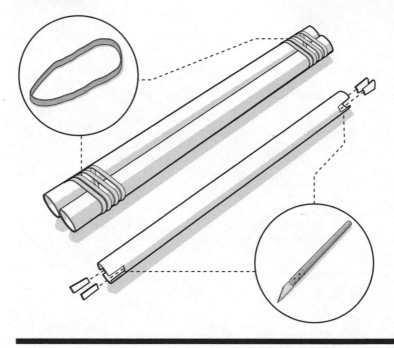

First, round up three plastic ballpoint pens. Using some elbow grease and possibly a tool or two, remove all the contents from the pen housings.

Use two of your thin elastic bands to bind two of the pen housings together. On the third pen housing, cut two small notches opposite one another on both ends. These notches will hold one wide elastic band.

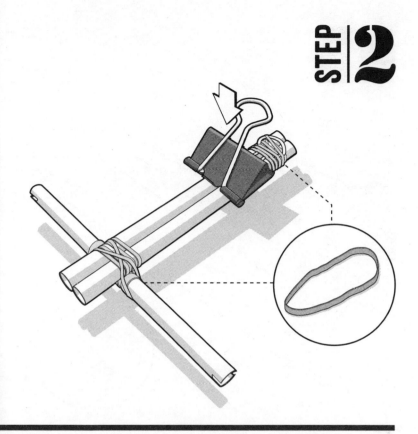

Now it's time for some light assembly. Start with the crossbow arm. Elastic band the third pen housing (with the notches) to the bottom of the double frame. You're looking for a 90-degree angle. Also, the notches on the third housing should be oriented parallel to the double frame, as shown.

Next, install a medium foldback clip to the back of the crossbow: Place the clip on the top of the double-pen frame, with clip end facing forwards, and use an elastic band to hold it in place. Only the bottom metal arm should be elastic banded – the top metal handle should remain free for loading and unloading the elastic band.

STEP 3

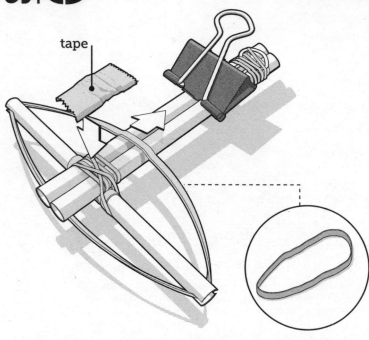

tape

Loop one wide elastic band through the pen housing grooves you cut earlier. Then pull back the band and clip it into the foldback clip. Cover the wrapped elastic band on the barrel with a single piece of tape to help smooth out the trajectory for your ammo.

Your Clip Crossbow is now in the fully drawn position until you release the foldback clip. Place the recommended rubber ammo in front of the clip before pressing the metal handle down. (See the final illustration on page 61 for placement.) Always wear safety glasses when firing the Clip Crossbow.

#2 CROSSBOW

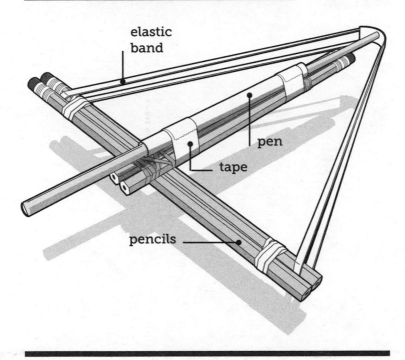

elastic band

pen

tape

pencils

The #2 Crossbow is a larger variant of the other bows found in this book. With a structurally solid design and double elastic power, it is equipped to fire large skewer arrows. It sports a pen-housing barrel that helps with both accuracy and control.

SUPPLIES

4 pencils
5 or 6 thin
   elastic bands
1 pen
Tape (any kind)
2 wide elastic bands

TOOLS

Safety glasses
Penknife (optional)
Pliers (optional)

AMMO

1+ wooden skewers
   (or 5mm dowels)

RANGE
6–12m

STEP 1

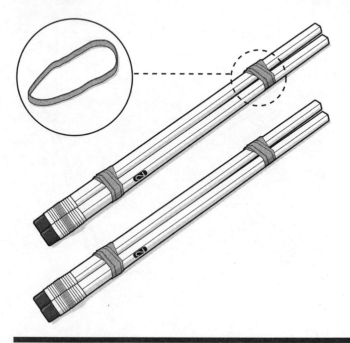

Using four thin elastic bands, tie two pairs of unsharpened wooden pencils as shown in the illustration. Both sets should be identical and tightly secured.

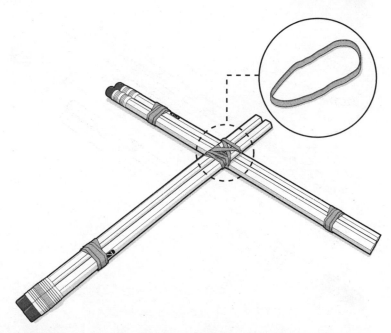

Crisscross the two sets of pencils. Centre one of the pairs on top of the other towards one end. This end will be the front of your #2 Crossbow. While holding the pairs in place, use one or two thin elastic bands to fasten the frames together.

STEP 3

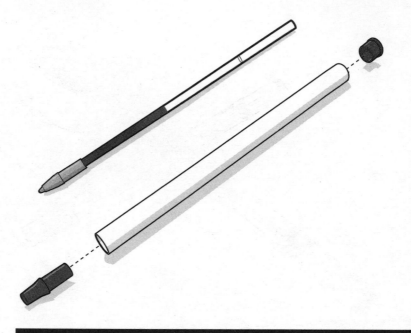

Dismantle a plastic ballpoint pen. You may need to use a pen-knife or pliers to remove the rear pen cap. The hollowed-out pen housing will be used for your crossbow barrel. Discard all the other pen contents (or save them to use for the Ruler Bow on page 73).

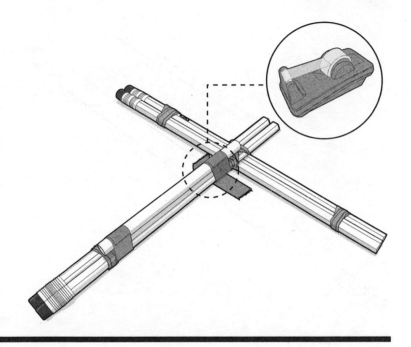

Position the pen housing on top of the pencils, as shown, then secure with tape. It is important that the pen housing sits on top of the elastic bands and that the barrel is not in any way obstructed by them.

Slide two wide elastic bands between the tightly secured pencil ends. The pencils should lock the bands in place, but if they don't, add additional thin elastic bands on the ends. The wide elastic bands will ultimately provide you with your elastic firepower.

Bring both ends of the elastic bands together and attach them using strong tape. As you secure the bands, try to create a small ammunition pouch with the tape. It is possible that you may need several pieces of tape to fasten the bands together securely. Pull the assembly back a few times with your finger to test it.

STEP 7

Your #2 Crossbow is now complete. Slide a wooden cooking skewer or a 5mm dowel into the pen housing. Gripping the wooden arrow and the elastic bands, pull back and aim your crossbow launcher. Release and watch it fly!

Always use your crossbow safely. Watch out for spectators and never aim the shooter at anyone. Wooden skewers usually have pointed tips, which can make them very dangerous. Styrofoam targets are ideal, but you should never place them in front of a breakable backdrop just in case you miss your target. Do not fire the #2 Crossbow if any of the elastic bands show signs of wear.

RULER BOW

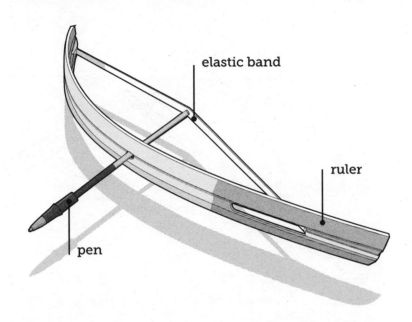

elastic band

ruler

pen

Every office has a modern-day Robin Hood, someone who steals office supplies from the rich and gives them to the poor. So if you want to play the part, you must arm yourself with the necessary archery hardware. This Ruler Bow is one of the most basic launchers known to humankind. In fact, it's not far off from the shooting stapler or spitballs. Despite its simplicity, it fires a great distance and is quite accurate.

SUPPLIES
1 elastic band
1 plastic ruler
  (with holes
  in each end)

TOOLS
Safety glasses
Scissors

AMMO
1 pen

RANGE
6–12m

>>>

STEP 1

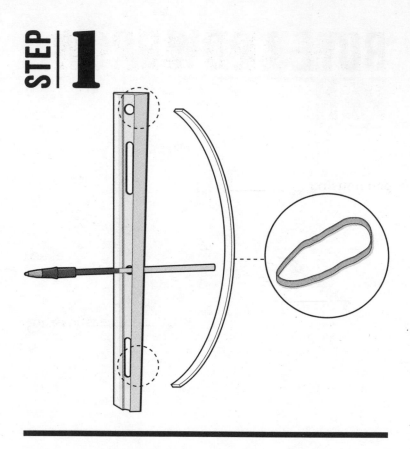

First, use scissors to sever a thick elastic band with one cut. Tie the elastic band to both ends of a plastic ruler through the factory holes moulded into it. A double or single knot will work just fine. (Metal or wooden rulers will also work for this project, but you may have to drill the holes yourself that are standard on most plastic rulers.)

Dismantle a plastic ballpoint pen. The interior pen tip will be your ammo. (You can save the housing for other Mini Weapons projects.)

Now you're ready for the hunt. Load the pen-tip arrow into the centre hole of the ruler, pull back the cartridge with the elastic band, and then release your ink missile by letting go of the elastic band.

BOW-AND-ARROW PEN

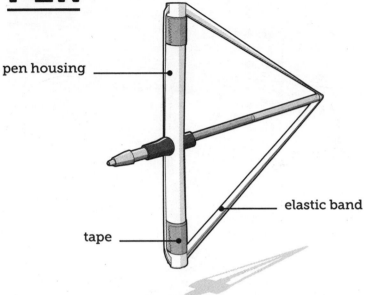

pen housing

elastic band

tape

Even Rambo needed a hobby. He mastered archery, and this sport can quickly occupy your time as well, while you perfect your mechanical principles. A customized plastic bow is ideal for long-distance competitions and target practice. Use the print-out targets in the back of the book to determine which of your fellow archers is the true Robin Hood.

SUPPLIES
1 wide elastic band
Duct tape

TOOLS
Safety glasses
Craft knife
Pliers (optional)

AMMO
1 pen

RANGE
2.5–6m

STEP 1

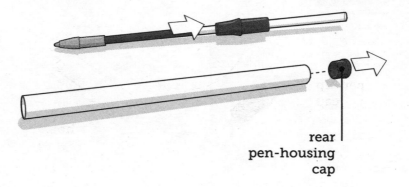

rear
pen-housing
cap

Disassemble a plastic ballpoint pen into its parts. Unless you chew on your pens, you may need a tool to dislodge the rear pen cap. A craft knife or small pliers should be sufficient. Lay out all the pen components and, unlike in previous builds, do not discard anything.

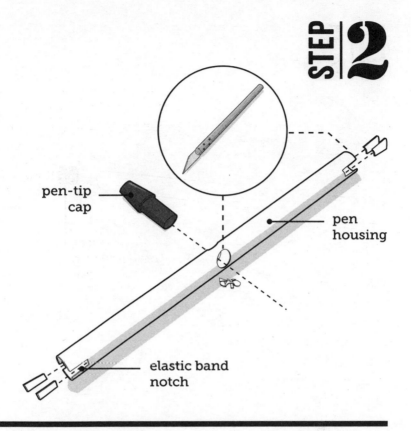

STEP|2

pen-tip cap

pen housing

elastic band notch

Using a craft knife, cut two circular openings in the centre of your pen housing directly across from each other. Your pen-tip cap should be able to fit snugly into the holes. Do not cut the holes too big – this will weaken the pen housing and could cause the frame to buckle later.

Next, cut two notches from each end of the housing. Notches should be aligned with the circular holes that you cut out for the pen tip, as shown.

STEP 3

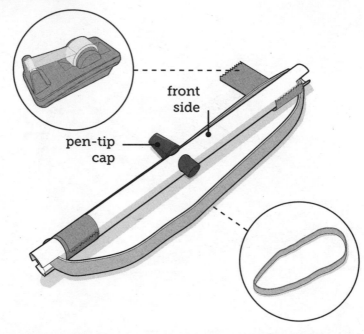

front side

pen-tip cap

Insert a wide elastic band into the end notches you created in the pen housing. Secure the elastic band with tape just next to each notch, but only tape the elastic band to the front side of the launcher. The back half of the band should not be taped in order to allow the elastic to bow.

Now insert the pen-tip cap into the holes made in the pen housing. This cap will support your ink arrows during firing. If the cap does not fit snugly, add tape for additional support. Move the elastic band up or down so it does not obstruct the hole in the pen-tip cap. You can tape it in place if you'd like.

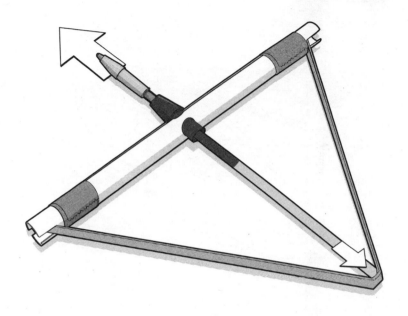

The Bow-and-Arrow Pen is now complete – time to fire it! Slide the ink cartridge through the pen-tip cap and grasp both the elastic band and the end of the ink cartridge to fire. Once the bow is drawn, release the elastic band and watch your ink arrow fly.

Remember that this homemade projectile launcher is capable of unfortunate malfunctions and misfires. Before firing, make sure to create a controlled shooting range in which to safely operate your weapon.

ALTERNATE CONSTRUCTION

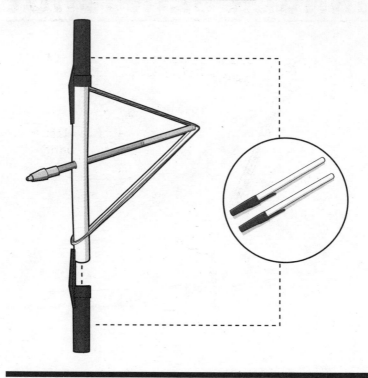

This version of the Bow-and-Arrow Pen substitutes two pen caps for the elastic band notches cut on both ends of the pen housing in the standard version. Slide the pen caps over the elastic band to secure the ends. You may add tape to help hold the caps in place. You will still need to disassemble your pen and cut a small hole in the centre of the pen housing for your ink arrow.

HANGER SLINGSHOT

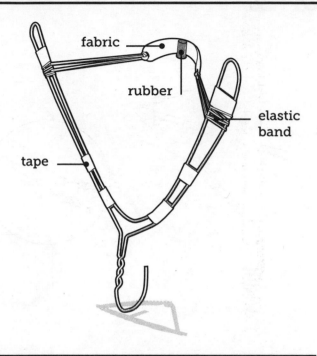

fabric

rubber

elastic band

tape

Every urban marksman needs a trusty slingshot, and with some perseverance you'll master this handheld catapult. This homemade slingshot has a solid steel frame and two powerful elastic strips for launching projectiles at high speeds. Good luck target hunting!

SUPPLIES

1 metal clothes
hanger
Masking or
duct tape
1 piece of fabric
4 elastic bands

TOOLS

Safety glasses
Scissors

AMMO

1+ rubber

RANGE

2.5–6m

STEP 1

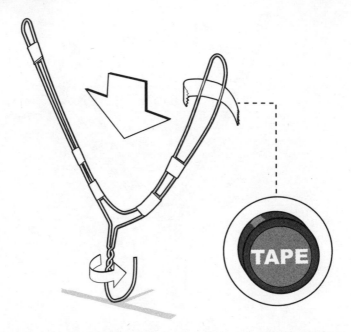

TAPE

Construct the Y-frame from a simple metal coat hanger by bending the bottom bar towards the hook. Once you've shaped your frame, wrap tape around several points on the hanger to prevent the frame from bending out of shape during firing.

Also, rotate the hanger's hook 90 degrees. This will become your slingshot handle.

Now it's time to make the slingshot pocket. Cut a small piece of fabric from an old flannel or tea towel. It should measure roughly 5cm by 1.5cm and have rounded corners. Use a small point to cut or poke a hole in both ends of the fabric.

Next, loop an elastic band through each hole and back through itself, as shown. This will create a knot when pulled.

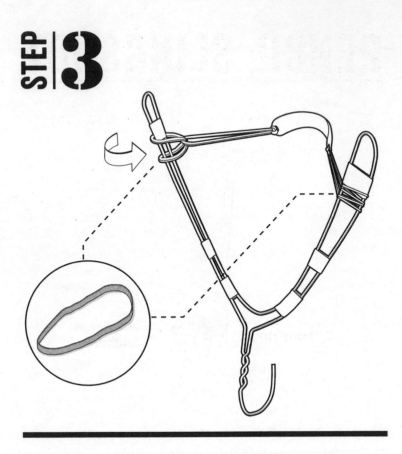

Use two more elastic bands to attach the power bands to the slingshot frame. Attach one elastic band per side, looping each through one of the elastic bands tied to the pouch. Then wrap each elastic band several times around its end of the metal frame. You may need to add tape or another elastic band to hold each firmly in place.

Once finished, pull back the pouch a few times to make sure everything feels secure. Now load your ammunition into the pouch, pull back and release. It is important that you do not draw the power bands directly back towards your eyes when firing. If the bands become hard, brittle or damaged, you should replace them. Remember to always wear safety glasses when shooting.

PENCIL SLINGSHOT

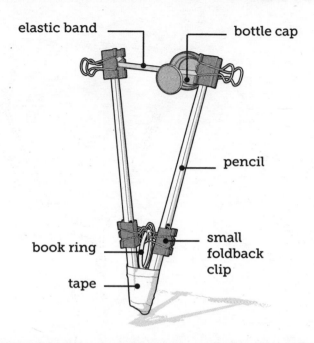

elastic band

bottle cap

pencil

book ring

small foldback clip

tape

This nifty little slingshot can be quickly assembled for early morning target practice. Its compact design is capable of shooting coins at incredible speeds. The Pencil Slingshot is also built to last and take abuse.

SUPPLIES

1 plastic bottle cap
1 wide elastic band
4 small foldback
  clips (19 mm)
2 pencils
1 book ring
Duct tape

TOOLS

Safety glasses
Craft knife

AMMO

1+ coins

RANGE

2.5–6m

STEP | 1

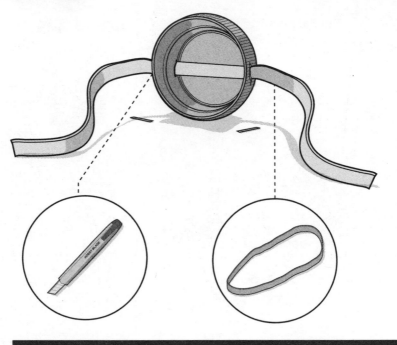

The first step is to construct the coin pouch. Use a craft knife to cut two slits through the opposite sides of a plastic bottle cap. The slits should be approximately the same length as the width of the elastic band.

Next, cut a wide elastic band open and slide it through the slits until the cap is centred.

7

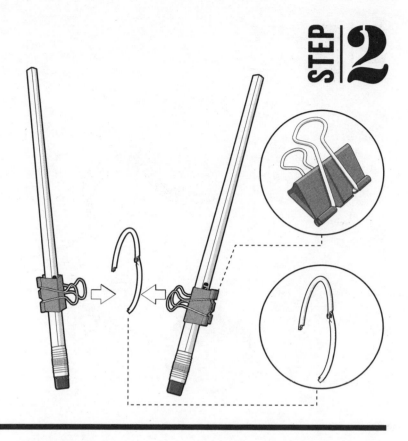

Now it's time to construct the Pencil Slingshot frame. Attach two small foldback clips to two unsharpened pencils, about halfway between the bottom and middle of each.

Next, loop a metal book ring through the two clips' metal handles and snap the book ring shut.

Next, secure the pencils together. Place the two pencil rubbers as shown, then tape them together. Try to prevent the pencils from overlapping and instead make sure that they are lined up; this will make for a stronger slingshot.

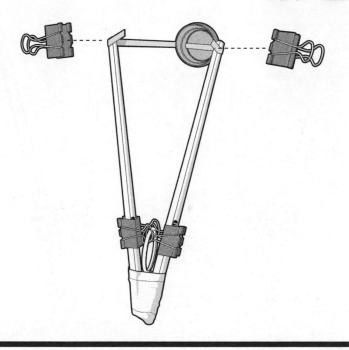

Now it's time to attach the power band to the two-pencil frame. Wrap one end of the elastic band around one of the pencil tips, then use a small foldback clip to secure it in place. Do the same for the other side. Once assembled, pull back the power band a few times to test the strength of the band and foldback clips. If your foldback clips do not hold the elastic band, use additional tape to secure them. Once everything is in working order, select a target and have fun!

3

DARTS

BUBBLE GUM DART

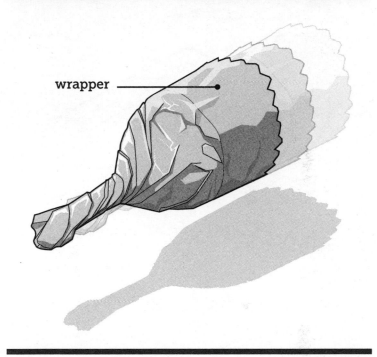

wrapper

The Bubble Gum Dart is a marvel of quick weaponry. Although it is only capable of travelling a distance of 3 metres or less, it takes mere seconds to construct, making it an absolute must for the avid chewer and skilled bubble-blowing assassin.

SUPPLIES

Chewing gum

TOOLS

Safety glasses
Your finger
Your mouth

AMMO

1+ gum wrapper

RANGE
1.8–3m

STEP 1

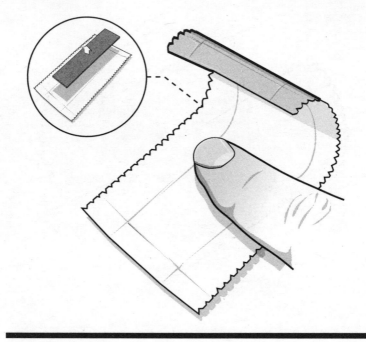

Locate an unused stick of gum. Flatten out the protective foil wrapper on a smooth surface, eliminating any folds or creases. Enjoy the gum.

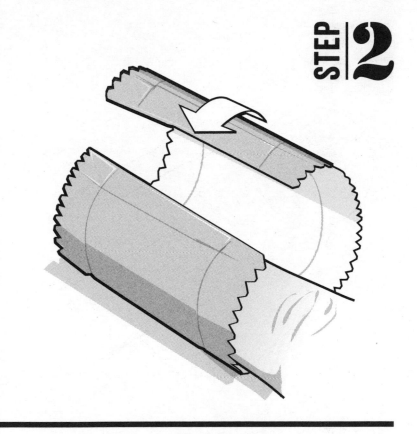

Position your finger in the centre of the foil, then roll the wrapper over your finger to construct a crude cylinder. It may not be rocket science... but it does build a simple rocket.

STEP 3

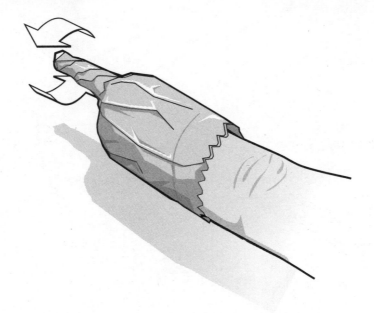

Now tightly twist the end of the wrapper in the same direction in which you wrapped it around your finger to form a point.

Slowly remove your finger from the cylinder. Place the Bubble Gum Dart in your mouth with only the tip protruding out between your lips, being careful not to crush the cylinder. Take a deep breath through your nose and then blow out through your mouth. Slowly open up your mouth as you exhale and watch the gum rocket fly across the room. The accuracy of these rockets varies, but you'll get better with practice. Never aim at another person.

SHOELACE DARTS

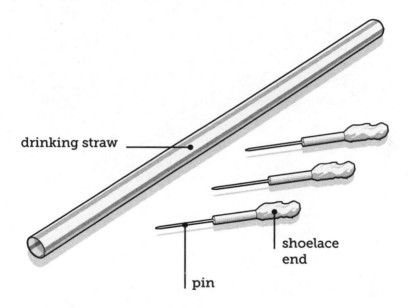

drinking straw

shoelace end

pin

Drinking straw to some, blowgun to others. This blowgun is capable of firing small needle-tipped darts with balloon-popping power! Unfortunately, you'll need someone to donate their shoelace ends to create this weapon.

SUPPLIES
1+ shoelaces
1+ pins
1 drinking straw

TOOLS
Safety glasses
Scissors
Pliers (optional)

AMMO
The constructed darts

RANGE
3–6m

STEP 1

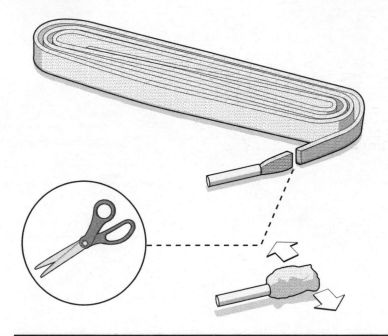

Your first plan of attack is to chop off the ends of someone's shoelaces. Take each detached end and use your fingers to fluff out the shoelace fabric while keeping together the plastic-tipped cylinder (also know as the aglet). This fluffed-out fabric will become your tail section and will help control the trajectory.

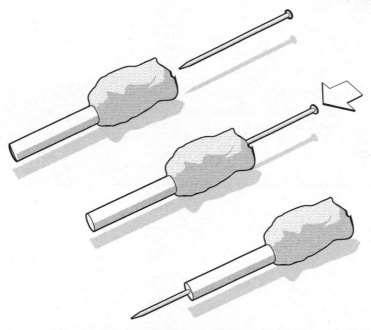

Now you must equip your dart with a point – a straight pin. Depending on how the shoelace was manufactured, you may run into a problem on this step; however, there are ways around it. The ideal method is to push the pin through the back tail section so that the point protrudes out of the end. If you find this difficult, you may want to use pliers to hold onto the lace to avoid poking your skin.

If the plastic aglet is too tight, change your approach: first poke a hole in the front end of the plastic aglet, then stick your pin in backwards. You will avoid having to burrow all the way through the tip, but the pin will be less secure.

Whatever method you decide to follow, your final product should be a tightly secured pin sticking out of the aglet end.

STEP 3

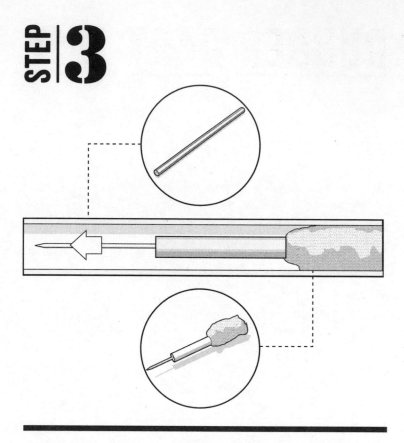

Now stuff your dart into a drinking straw with the point facing towards the exit. Aim the straw and hold it to your lips. Then take a deep breath and exhale sharply to blow the dart out.

It is very important to remember that you're firing needles from your mouth. *You should never inhale while the straw is in your mouth waiting to be launched.* Always be responsible and fire it in a controlled manner. *Safety glasses are a must, as is staying clear of spectators.*

RUBBER DART

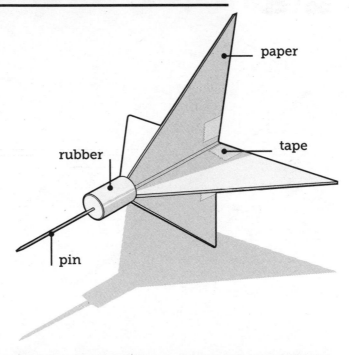

paper

tape

rubber

pin

The Rubber Dart is the official dart of the little-known National Rubber Dart Association (NRDA). Because NRDA is so very secretive, you're encouraged to make up your own rules, and with such loose standards, starting a NRDA league is simple and fun. The only requirements for a tournament are to always throw at a makeshift dartboard, not at one another, and to keep all players behind a throwing line marked on the floor.

SUPPLIES

1 sheet of paper
1 pencil rubber
1 pin
Transparent tape

TOOLS

Safety glasses
Scissors
Penknife

AMMO

The constructed dart

RANGE

3–6m

>>>

STEP 1

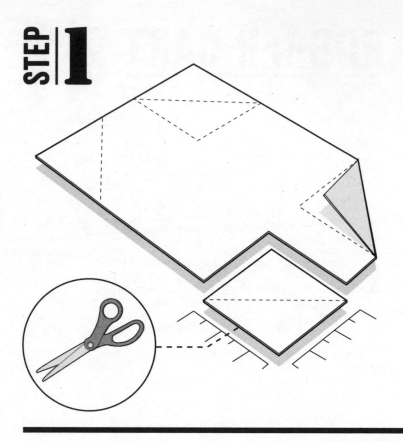

First, construct the tail of the Dart. Using a normal-sized sheet of paper, fold up one of the corners to be approximately 6cm by 6cm. This will form a square once it's unfolded.

After you have made a perfect folded square, cut it out. This is all the paper you will need to make one Rubber Dart; save the rest of the paper to make additional darts later.

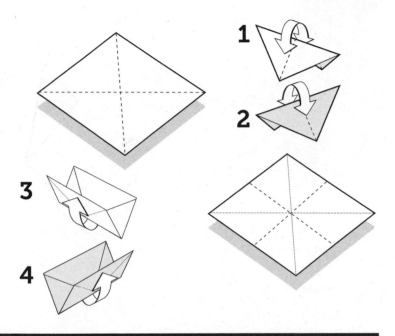

Now that you have a perfect square, you will need to add some additional folds. This step is similar to the Water Bomb assembly found in chapter 6 (page 201). First, fold opposite corners of the paper together to form two triangles, then unfold the paper and fold the other two corners together to form two triangles, as shown above.

Next, fold the paper in half both ways. Once you have finished you should have folded the paper a total of four times and should have four crease lines as shown above. These creases will act as guides for the major folds in the next step.

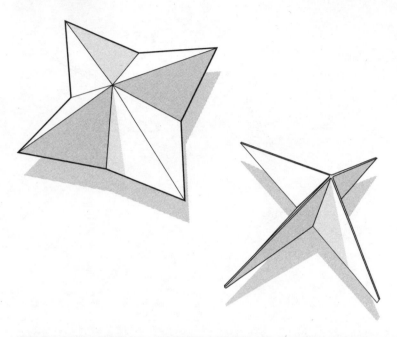

Now, creatively folding your square, push up on the centre point and down on the middles of the sides until you have what appears to be a star. This may take a few attempts due to the confusing nature of the creases. Use the illustration above for reference.

Once you've completed the folds, run your fingers along the fold lines to crease the edges. This will help the paper keep its form during construction.

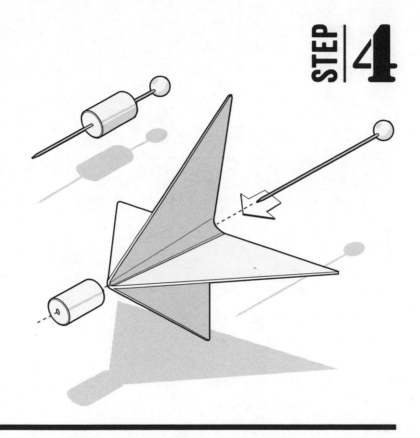

Cut a new rubber off a pencil using a penknife. Then prepare the rubber by pushing a pin through the centre of it and removing it again.

Now open up the rear section of the paper fins. From the back, push the pointed end of the pin through the centre point of the paper fins. (A standard straight pin with a round head is ideal for this dart design. A smaller pinhead will ultimately fall out of the front of the paper fins and cause failure.) Once through the paper, push the pin back through the hole you made in the centre of your rubber. Make sure the head of the pin is tight against the rubber for a solid assembly.

RUBBER DART

STEP 5

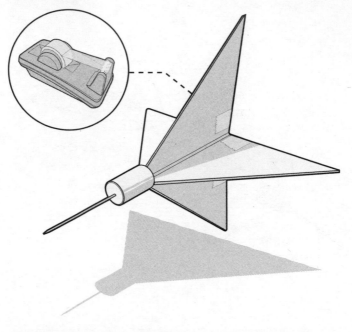

Your dart is almost complete – just tape the backs of the wings together so that the Rubber Dart keeps its shape when flying across the room.

Safety first! Your mini javelin should travel with enough force to stick into a cork or wooden target, but these Rubber Darts are not toys and should never be thrown at human or animal targets. It is important that you aim at a large target area away from spectators when launching your darts. Remember, because these darts are homemade, accuracy is likely to vary.

LONG DART

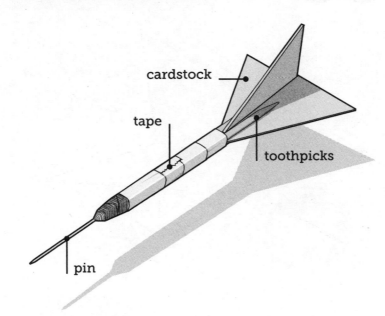

cardstock

tape

toothpicks

pin

Long Darts are designed for speed, distance, and accuracy. These micro-arrows are perfect for competitive activities, such as traditional pub darts. Because they cost very little to build, accumulating many for friendly homemade games is no problem at all. Don't have a dartboard? Chapter 7 (page 222) has a perfect one for you to use.

SUPPLIES
4 toothpicks
Masking tape
1 small metal pin
Thread
Glue (optional)
Cardboard

TOOLS
Safety glasses
Scissors

AMMO
The constructed dart

RANGE
3–6m

STEP |1

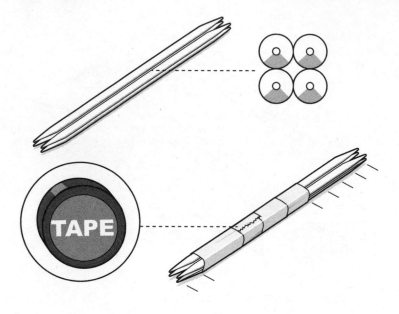

Tightly tape together four round toothpicks to form a square bundle as shown. It is important to leave the back half of the bundle untaped so that you can slide the cardboard fins into place later.

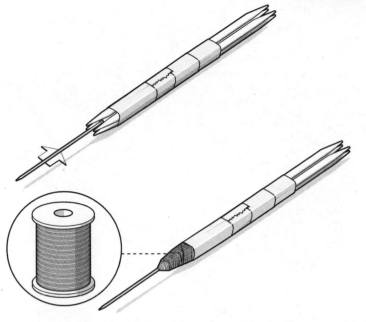

Now take a small metal pin and wedge it into the front centre of the four toothpicks. A pin with a small head or a small finishing nail works best. Once in place, tightly wrap the front of the dart with thread. Continue to wrap it until your point is immovable and secure.

You may dab some glue onto the thread wrapping to bond it further. Allow 30 minutes for the glue to dry.

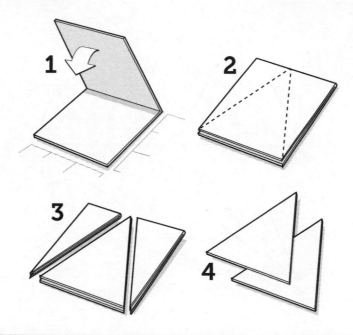

Now it's time to construct the Long Dart's fins. Use thin cardboard of the sort found on most cereal and cracker boxes. Once you have removed a section of cardboard from the box, cut out a 7.5cm by 4cm rectangle. Then fold that rectangle in half to create a 4cm by 4cm double square. The square will be two cardboard layers thick. This will ensure that the four fins are the exact same size after you cut them out.

Now use scissors to cut out a triangle shape, as shown above, from your folded cardboard. Remove the extra material from both sides. When finished, you should end up with two triangles of exactly the same size. The triangles should be separate, not connected at the tip.

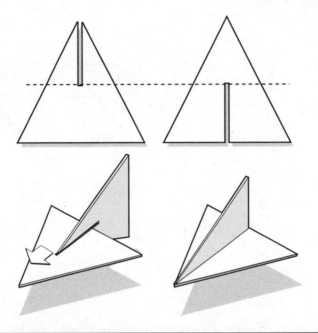

Place the two separate cardboard triangles side by side.

On the first triangle, use scissors to cut out a small slit from the top point of the triangle to about halfway down. The width of the slit should be the same as the thickness of the cardboard, but not bigger. On the second triangle, cut out a small slit of the same width from the midpoint of the bottom edge to approximately halfway up the triangle.

Now slide the two triangles together as shown to form the rear fin assembly.

Now it's time to introduce the two parts you have created to one another. Slide the fins into the four-toothpick assembly from behind, so that one fin is wedged between each tooth-pick pair. The pressure of the toothpicks will hold the fins in place when in use. The Long Dart is now complete and ready for bull's-eye practice.

It is important to remember that your dart has a dangerous point at the end and is not meant for throwing at living targets. Malfunctions do also occur, so exercise the utmost caution when launching your homemade darts. Always use common sense, and use at your own risk. A dartboard layout, perfect for target practice, is located on page 222.

PAPER DARTS

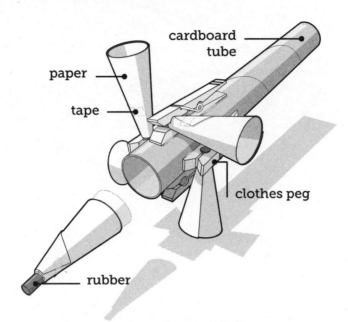

cardboard tube

paper

tape

clothes peg

rubber

The Paper Dart is the perfect indoor launcher for a friendly game of tag. Armed with several darts, you can quickly reload and refire while on the offensive. Its quick construction and harmless darts make this Mini Weapon a must for any rainy day! Plus, once you learn the basic fundamentals of the blow-gun, you can easily adapt it to other designs.

SUPPLIES
1 sheet of paper
Transparent tape
1 cardboard tube
4+ pushpins
4+ pencil rubbers
4 clothes pegs

TOOLS
Safety glasses
   (if playing
   Paper-Dart Tag)
Scissors
Penknife
Hot glue gun

AMMO
The constructed
   darts

RANGE
3–6m

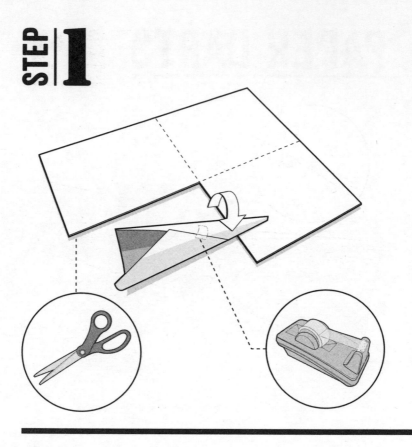

Take a standard sheet of paper and divide it into four equal sections by folding it twice. Once you have created your fold lines, cut out the sections with scissors. Next, take one paper section and roll it into a funnel. Use tape to hold the paper in place, and then make three more funnels in the same way with the remaining paper.

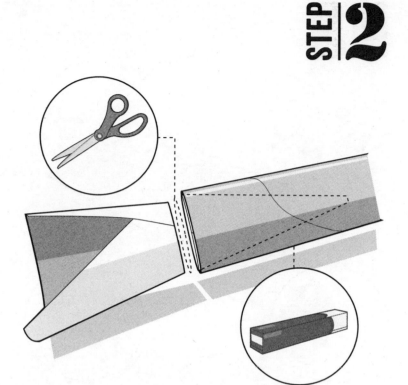

Select a smaller cardboard tube with which to construct your blowgun housing. An aluminium foil or plastic-wrap tube from the kitchen will work best; avoid wider tubes as they will dramatically decrease the firing distance of your Paper Dart.

Stick one of the paper funnels into the tube, being careful not to damage it. Once it's gently wedged into the tube, use scissors to trim off the extra material hanging out of the tube. Now your dart's maximum width is the exact size of the tube's diameter, which will increase the contact surface area when you blow through the tube.

STEP 3

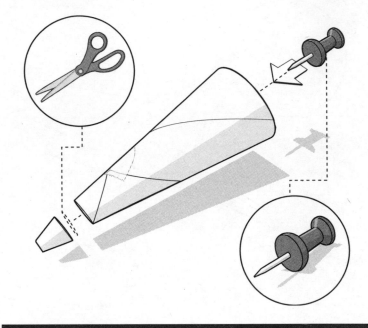

Remove the paper funnel from the tube. Trim off the nose of your paper funnel with scissors, just enough so that a pushpin will not fall out when placed inside.

Load a pushpin from the rear of the paper funnel with the metal point entering first. Tip the paper cone so that the push-pin slides all the way to the front of the cone. If the pin falls out of the front, your hole may be too large.

x4

Cut the rubber off a pencil using a penknife. With the tip of your pushpin protruding out of the paper cone, fold the paper inwards around the metal point. Once all the paper is pushed down around the metal point, slide the pencil rubber onto the pin tip. Push the rubber as far back as possible to sandwich the pushed-down paper between the rubber and pushpin.

If you want multiple darts, repeat these steps until you've accumulated a stockpile of ammunition. This Paper Dart gun can hold four darts while firing one.

STEP 5

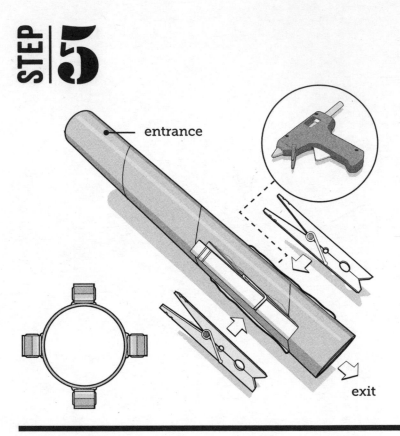

entrance

exit

Your Paper Dart launcher is now fully functional without these additional steps; however, these improvements will impress your friends and frighten your enemies.

Using a hot glue gun, glue four clothes pegs to the firing end of your cardboard tube. They should be evenly spaced around the tube and an equal distance from the end. See the illustration for the pattern. Be careful to only glue the bottom wooden prong – the clip should still be functional.

STEP | 6

During combat, the ammo clips will make it easier to safely transport your paper darts and will be a great reminder of how many shots you have remaining.

To fire, load one dart into the rear of the tube (rubber end first) and exhale into the tube as hard as you can with a quick burst of air. Your darts will be launched across the room with a surprising amount of accuracy.

Remember to always inspect your darts to make sure the pushpin is properly wedged into the rubber.

4

CATAPULTS

CLOTHES PEG CATAPULT

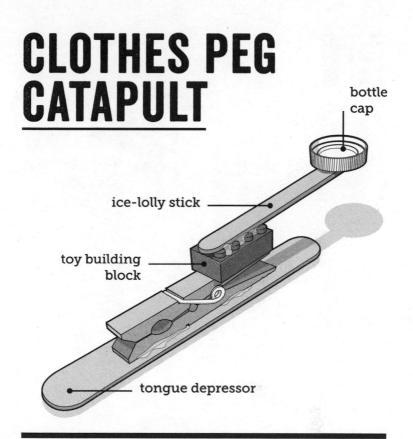

bottle cap

ice-lolly stick

toy building block

tongue depressor

This is a very simple catapult with endless possibilities for fun. It will only take a few seconds to glue and assemble, but finding a toy building block may take a bit longer. If you can't find one in the toy box, I suggest looking under the bed or behind the sofa cushions.

SUPPLIES

1 toy building block
   (2 peg by 4 peg)
1 clothes peg
1 tongue depressor
1 bottle cap
1 ice-lolly stick

TOOLS

Safety glasses
Hot glue gun

AMMO

1+ small
   marshmallows
1+ pencil rubbers

RANGE

3–6m

STEP | 1

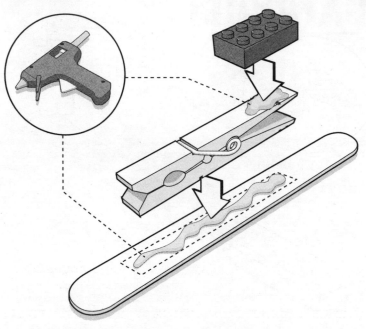

You'll need a 2-peg-by-4-peg toy building block (or something equivalent in mass and size) for this step. Using your hot glue gun, affix a clothes peg to a wooden tongue depressor; then attach the toy brick onto the back end of the clothes peg's top prong. The clothes peg should remain fully functional.

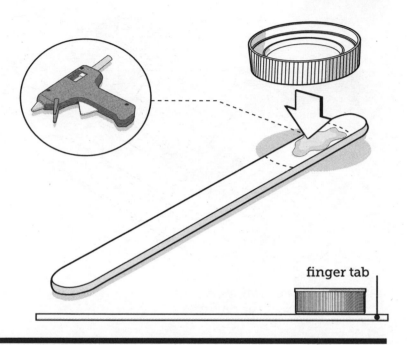

finger tab

If you successfully operated the glue gun without burning yourself in the last step, here is another opportunity to do some damage. Glue a plastic bottle cap from a soft drink bottle to one end of a wooden ice-lolly stick, but leave a small tab at the end of the stick for your finger. This finger tab will come in handy when you begin your siege and have to quickly launch a hailstorm of ammunition.

CLOTHES PEG CATAPULT

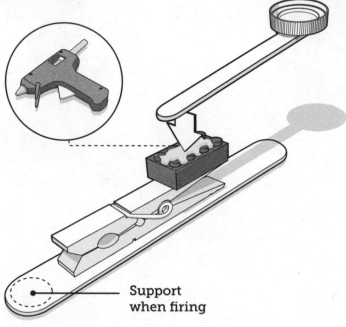

Support
when firing

With your poor burnt fingers, combine the two assemblies to complete your Clothes Peg Catapult. Lay a small amount of hot glue onto the top of the building block and then carefully push the ice-lolly stick onto the brick.

Wait a few minutes for your glue to cool before test firing. Always wear safety glasses while operating a catapult. Small marshmallows or pencil rubbers are the ideal ammunition for these contraptions. Substitution of more serious ammunition could cause harm. Use at your own risk.

DEPRESSOR CATAPULT

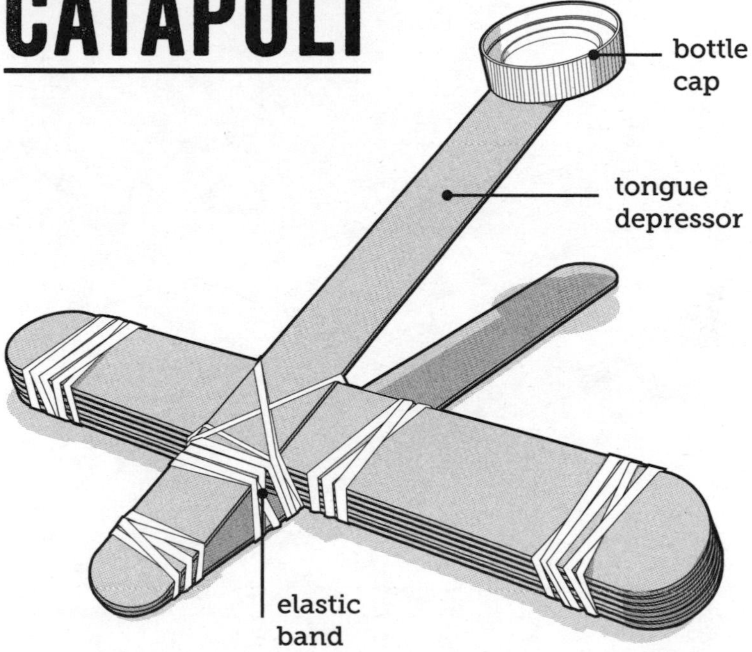

bottle cap

tongue depressor

elastic band

This cut-rate catapult is perfect for mass production and outdoor use.

SUPPLIES
9 tongue depressors
7 elastic bands
1 bottle cap

TOOLS
Safety glasses
Hot glue gun

AMMO
1+ pencil rubbers

RANGE
3–6m

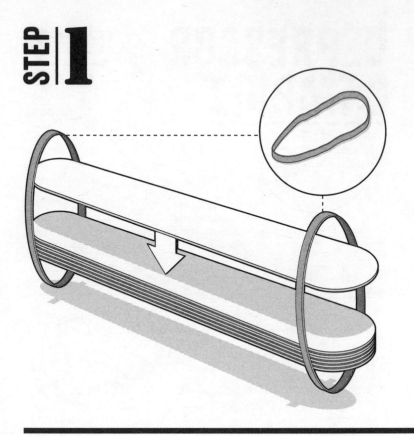

You will need seven wooden depressors in total for this step. Stack them on top of one another as neatly as possible before elastic banding them together at the ends.

Gluing them in this step would also work, though it will take some time.

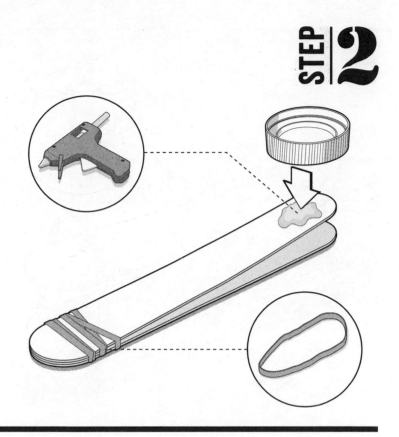

Take two additional tongue depressors and elastic band them together at one end.

Next, take a plastic cap from a soft-drink bottle and hot glue it to the end of one of the tongue depressors, opposite the end held together by elastic bands. Now your catapult arm is finished. Note: If you substitute ice-lolly sticks for tongue depressors they will eventually snap in half because of their thickness. They will work, but not for long.

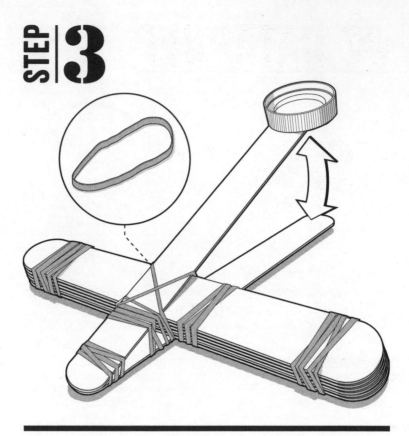

Before you can unleash catapulting terror on your targets, you must assemble the hinge arm. Slide the depressor bundle between the two tongue depressors from step 2 as shown. The tension of the arm assembly will force the bundle backwards; use elastic bands to stop this and to hold it in place.

Now your catapult is complete. With one hand, hold the seven-depressor base on either side as you load the bottle cap. Pull down the top arm assembly to launch a soft projectile.

#2 CATAPULT

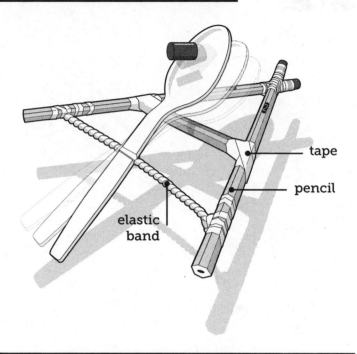

tape

pencil

elastic
band

The #2 Catapult is a great on-the-go siege machine. In order to fire it, you have to be holding it in your hand – no surface required. Once you've mastered the ideal trajectory angle, the catapult can be quite accurate.

SUPPLIES

3 wooden pencils
3 wide elastic bands
Masking or duct tape
1 plastic spoon

TOOLS

Safety glasses
Penknife

AMMO

1+ pencil rubbers

RANGE
3–6m

STEP 1

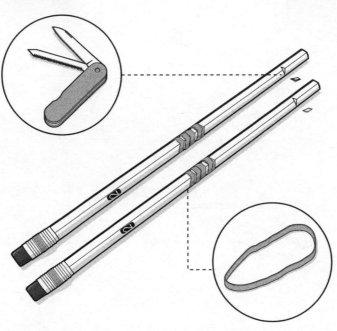

First, prepare two wooden pencils. Twist one elastic band around the centre of each of the pencils until tight. You may have to first twist each band at the pencil end and then slide it down to the centre.

Next, take a penknife and notch out two small grooves about half an inch from the non-rubber ends, as shown.

Attach the two modified pencils together with an elastic band at the rubber ends in a way that is flexible enough to create a V-shaped frame, as in the illustration above.

Take a third pencil and cut off the rubber. Then cut the rest of the pencil into two segments, one of which is 7.5cm long. Clean up the cut edges with the penknife. The 7.5-cm segment will act as a spacer in the next step; set aside the remaining segment for later.

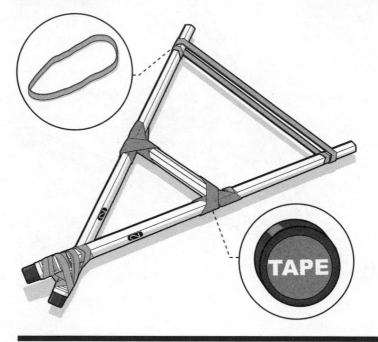

TAPE

Tape this segment in place while it's resting on the elastic bands. The bands should add additional support and help the frame keep its structure.

Next, wrap one large, wide elastic band around the ends of the pencil near the two notches you cut out earlier. Just loop the elastic band a few times until it stays in place. Add additional elastic bands to hold it in place if needed.

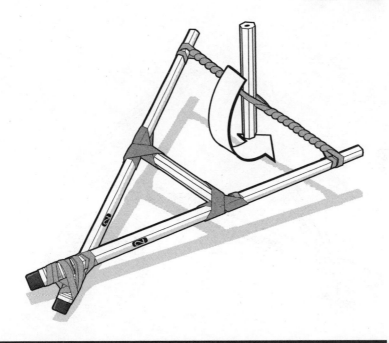

Now take the leftover section of the third pencil and slide it between the two sides of the thick elastic band you just installed. Once it's in place, use the pencil segment to spin and coil the elastic band. This stored energy will be the power source of the catapult. Once you feel you've created enough elastic energy, *do not let go!*

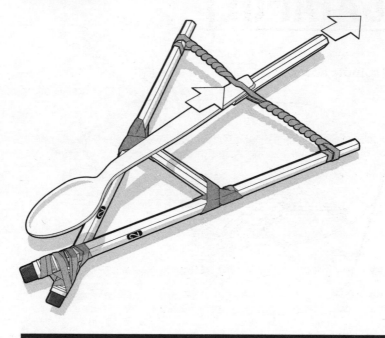

Now for the hard part. Slowly slide a plastic spoon handle through the elastic band opening, as shown. Once the spoon is in place, remove the pencil segment, and you're ready to go.

While holding the launcher, pull back the spoon, load a rubber, and let it rip. When operating, wear safety glasses and always prepare for the unexpected. Never fire ammo that can cause harm to another individual. If the elastic band starts to show signs of wear, replace it before using the catapult again.

CD-SPINDLE CATAPULT

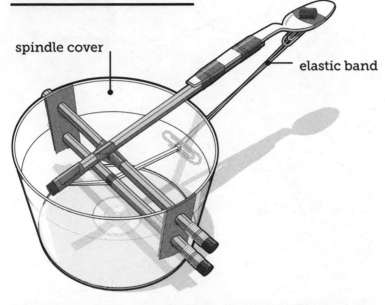

spindle cover

elastic band

The CD-Spindle Catapult not only fires ammunition, but can store your shots as well. This project calls for a CD-spindle cap to use as the base; however, a shoebox or other smaller-sized container will also work if a CD spindle is not available.

SUPPLIES
1 CD-spindle cover
Masking tape
2 paper clips
1 plastic spoon
3 wooden pencils
2 elastic bands

TOOLS
Safety glasses
Craft knife

AMMO
1+ mini
    marshmallows

RANGE
3–6m

STEP | 1

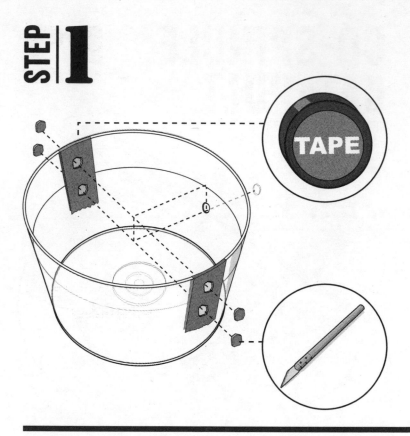

TAPE

Take a CD-spindle cover and lay two pieces of masking tape directly across from one another on the inside and outside of the plastic surface. (This will help control the brittle plastic when you are cutting your holes.) Now take your craft knife and cut a series of five pencil-sized holes into the plastic cover. Two sets should be exactly across from one another on the tape you stuck on earlier. The fifth hole should be cut midway between them at the same height as the bottom hole. Refer to the illustration above for the proper placement. Holes should not be cut close to the bottom.

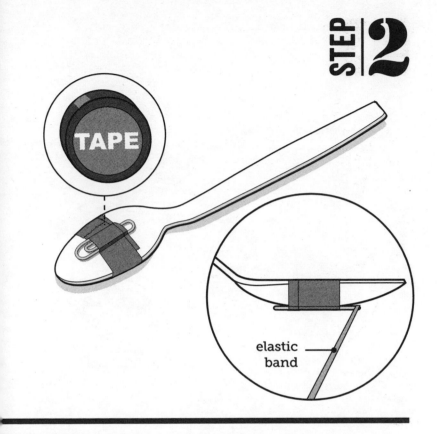

TAPE

elastic
band

Next, construct the arm that will help you hurl objects across the room. Tape a standard paper clip to the belly of your plastic spoon. Later on, this paper clip will become your elastic band trigger, but you will not be putting an elastic band on it at this point. The illustration here is just for future reference.

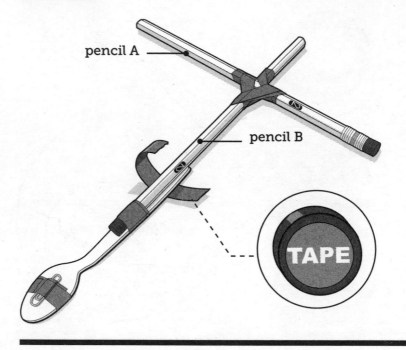

pencil A

pencil B

TAPE

You will now complete the catapult arm with two wooden pencils and the spoon assembly from the previous step. Place pencil B in the centre of pencil A (roughly three-quarters of the way down pencil B), as shown. Once in place, tape the two pencils together. You can substitute an elastic band for the tape, but be sure to refer to the illustration for positioning.

Now fasten the plastic spoon onto the long end of pencil B. Tape in multiple spots to keep the spoon from becoming loose, which could reduce the power and accuracy of your catapult.

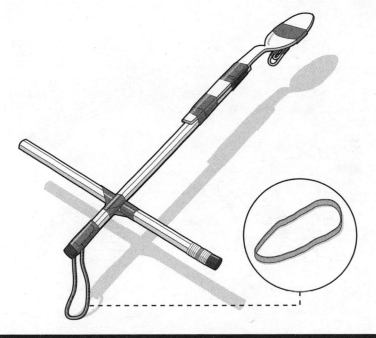

Tape an elastic band to the bottom of pencil B at the end opposite the spoon. The elastic band will provide the power for your catapult, so should be unused and without cracks.

This type of catapult is referred to as a torsion engine. A real torsion engine catapult would use treated twine or twisted rope to provide its wall-smashing power.

CD-SPINDLE CATAPULT

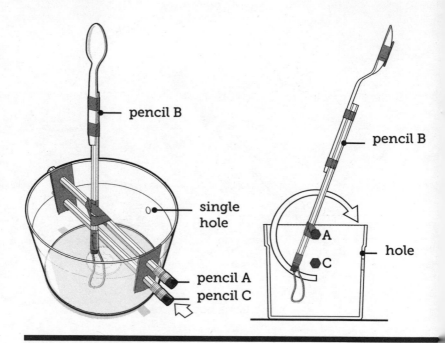

Now, from the inside of the spindle cover, delicately slide pencil A into the top two holes that you cut out earlier. Note that pencil B should not be touching the bottom of the container when vertical.

Next, slide in pencil C. This pencil will prevent the arm from swinging towards the ground, which would propel your ammunition into the ground as well.

Pencil B should be the farthest away from the single hole when vertical. See the illustration.

Now looking at the catapult from the opposite side. Pull the elastic band attached to pencil B through the single hole and secure it to a paper clip on the other side of the plastic. This will prevent the elastic band from breaking free and disabling your siege weapon.

Your catapult should work at this stage; however, you will find it difficult to hold, load and fire all at the same time. The next step illustrates how to use the elastic band trigger you installed earlier on the plastic spoon.

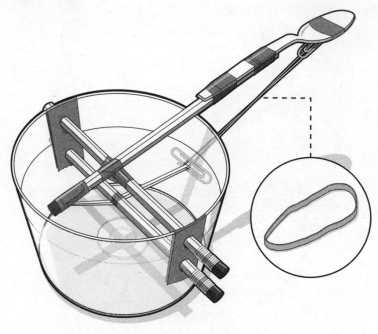

Loop an elastic band around both paper clips you installed earlier. This will keep the catapult in the locked position, perfect for loading and aiming. Once you have loaded your chosen ammunition, use your finger to flick the elastic band connection off the spoon. Just remember to use your other hand to support the base when firing.

The CD spindle's cover works well for mini marshmallow battles. Use your opponent's cover for a scoring basket when testing your skills.

SIEGE CATAPULT

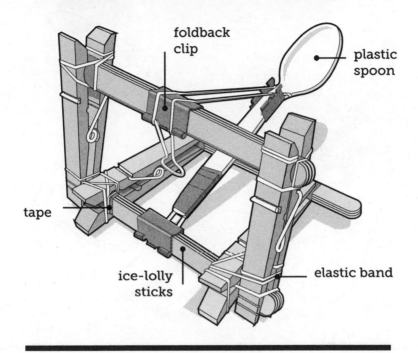

- foldback clip
- plastic spoon
- tape
- ice-lolly sticks
- elastic band

Not only is this a true torsion engine catapult, it even looks like its real-life big brother. This catapult can be built very cheaply, which makes it great for producing in mass quantities.

SUPPLIES

9 ice-lolly sticks
Masking or duct tape
4 clothes pegs
7+ elastic bands
3 small foldback
    clips (19 mm)
1 plastic spoon

TOOLS

Safety glasses

AMMO

1+ mini
    marshmallows

RANGE
3–6m

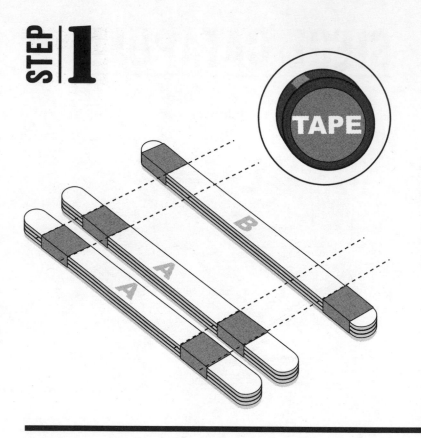

First, bundle up your ice-lolly sticks. Take nine sticks and divide them up into three piles – two A piles and one B pile. Each pile should be three sticks high.

Begin by taping both A piles about 1.5cm from their ends. Pile B should be taped just before the round ends on the sticks, as illustrated above.

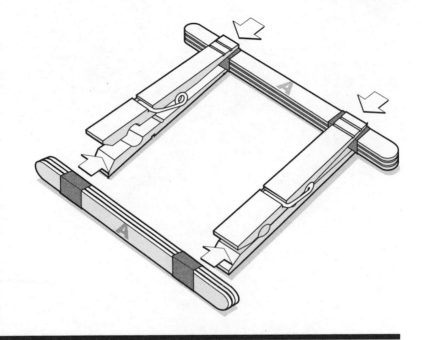

Next, take one of the A piles and clip it into two wooden clothes pegs. The clothes pegs should be positioned on the tape, and the ice-lolly sticks should be vertical. Then slide the second A pile horizontally between the clothes peg prongs at the rear of the clothes pegs. Refer to the illustration.

The taped areas should help hold the final frame in place when the catapult is being operated.

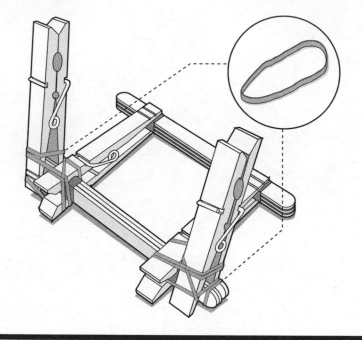

Next, take two wooden clothes pegs and slide the prongs between the ice-lolly sticks in the vertical bundle as illustrated. You'll have to muscle the ice-lolly sticks apart in order to fit each clothes peg prong between them.

Now strap the two clothes pegs in place with an elastic band at each end. Once you feel the clothes pegs are secure, move on to the next step. If you want to add additional elastic band support to the rear, please do so.

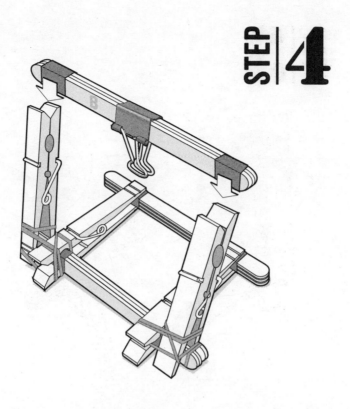

Take a small foldback clip and clamp it to the centre of the third bundle of sticks – pile B. This is the pile with the tape at the ends.

Now clip the bundle into the upright clothes pegs, making sure to line the clothes pegs up with the tape. The ice-lolly sticks in the bundle should be vertical and the foldback clip's metal handles should face down, as shown in the illustration.

STEP 5

TAPE

Now it's time to construct the plastic hurling arm with two more small foldback clips and a plastic spoon.

First, take a foldback clip and tape one of its metal handles to the underside of the handle end of the plastic spoon, as shown. (Do not remove the second metal handle on this clip.)

Next, attach another foldback clip to the underside of the spoon's neck. Squeeze both metal handles from the sides to release. (Foldback clips vary by manufacturer, so if you are unable to remove the handles, you may have to skip attaching the foldback clip to the neck and instead tape the elastic band onto the spoon in step 7.)

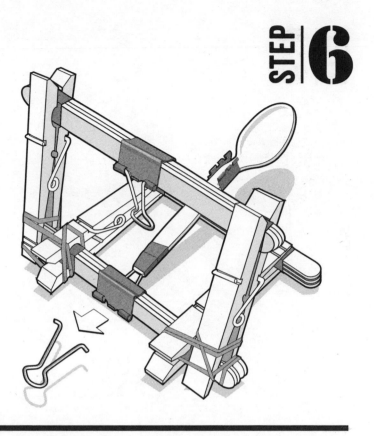

Now, use the foldback clip attached to the spoon handle to clip the spoon onto the lower craft-stick brace. The clip should be centred on the brace. Once the spoon is in place, remove the front metal handle of the foldback clip.

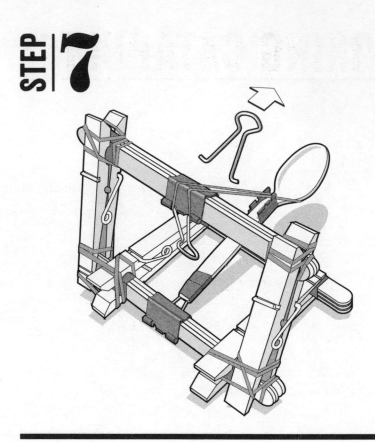

Now loop a small elastic band around the neck of the plastic spoon. Position the elastic band so it runs through the clip attached to the spoon's neck. This clip will hold the elastic band in position.

Loop the other end of the elastic band around the fold-back clip located on the top craft-stick bundle. Wedge it under the metal handle on the clip, and if necessary, clip it under the foldback clip to hold it in place. Now remove the back metal handle on this clip (the handle on the side facing the plastic spoon), and you're ready to launch.

Remember the importance of safety when operating your Siege Catapult. Never aim it at another human or animal and only use safe ammunition. Mini marshmallows work nicely.

VIKING CATAPULT

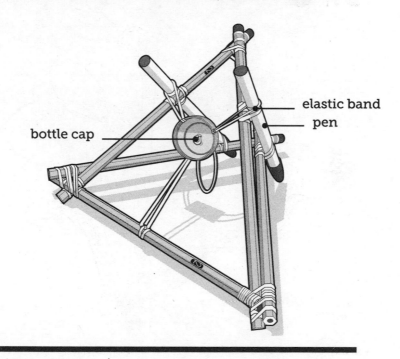

bottle cap

elastic band
pen

The Viking Catapult is a practical tabletop siege weapon with unlimited ammo possibilities — capable of launching rubbers, marshmallows, coins and much more. With an intimidating silhouette and a straightforward firing mechanism, it's the perfect machine to inflict physical damage on any target.

SUPPLIES
5 wooden pencils
14+ elastic bands
2 plastic pens
1 bottle cap

TOOLS
Safety glasses
Craft knife

AMMO
1+ pencil rubbers
(can be taken from
the frame's pencils)

RANGE
4.5–9m

STEP 1

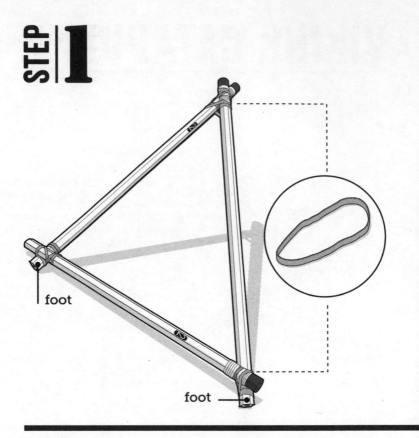

foot

foot

First, rummage through your desk drawers and select three wooden pencils. Use them to construct a triangular frame, securing the connections with elastic bands. You will have some overhang at the ends; these will become your feet.

Next, take two more pencils and lash them together at one end using an elastic band or two, similar to the construction of the #2 Catapult on page 127.

The connection should be tight enough to hold the pencils together but loose enough to bend them into a V shape for the next step. This assembly will make up half of the finished Viking Catapult.

STEP 3

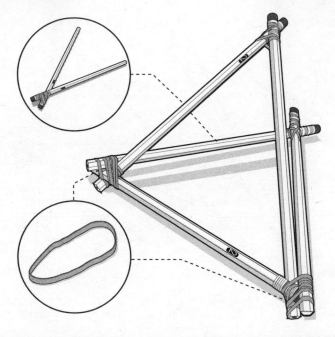

You will now combine the two assemblies from steps 1 and 2 to form a single frame. Take the two-pencil assembly and bend the pencils outward into a V shape. Rest the unattached ends of the two pencils onto the three-pencil triangular frame. Once in place, elastic band the two assemblies together to hold them in position.

This step will complete your frame. Take two pens and place them on the sides of the triangle on the top halves of the pencils. Secure them in place with elastic bands.

Next, position the ends of the pens towards the back of the V-shaped pencil frame. Place the pens so they extend below the triangle base and become feet for the catapult. Once in place, use elastic bands to secure them in place.

The pens can be adjusted later to change the trajectory of the catapult.

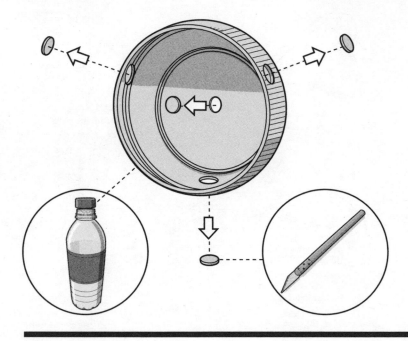

Now take a plastic cap from a soft drink bottle. Use a craft knife to cut four small holes into the cap. The first hole will be dead centre in the top. This hole should be approximately the same width as the elastic band you will use in step 6. The remaining three holes should be equally spaced around the side of the bottle cap, as shown.

Avoid getting too close to the edge of the bottle cap when cutting your holes. Insufficient material may mean that your catapult gives way when used, resulting in malfunctions.

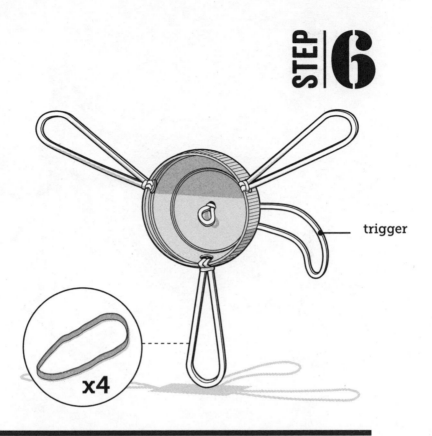

trigger

x4

Loop one elastic band through each side hole and then over the cap and back through itself to form a knot. Each elastic band will then form a loop coming from the bottle cap.

The elastic band in the centre should be pulled through the hole and then tied into a small knot on the inside of the cap. The knot must be considerably larger than the hole in the centre of the bottle cap to prevent the elastic band from being yanked out.

STEP 7

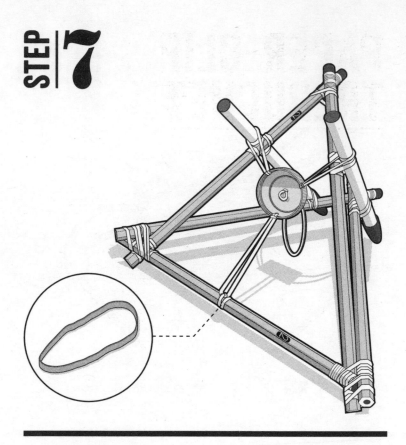

It is now time to install your bottle cap assembly onto its Viking Catapult frame.

Two of the elastic bands attached to the side of the bottle cap should be looped over the pens. Position the bottle cap so that these two elastic bands come from the upper part of the cap; the third elastic band should hang straight down. Depending on the length of these elastic bands, you may want to wrap them a few times to tighten the connection. Pull the third elastic band, hanging off the bottom of the bottle cap, down towards the lower pencil and fasten it with an elastic band. That elastic band should be centred on the base pencil.

Now load your bottle cap with ammunition, pull back the centred elastic band attached to the back of the bottle cap and release. If needed, adjust the pens for a better launch angle.

PAPER-CLIP
TREBUCHET

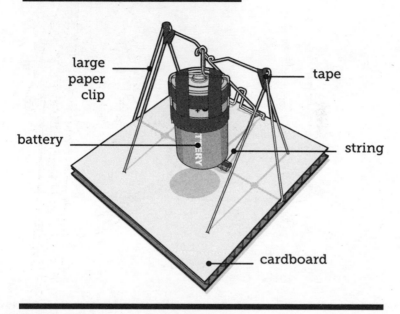

large paper clip

tape

battery

string

cardboard

The counterweight trebuchet is a siege weapon dating back to the Middle Ages. It was designed to launch projectiles hundreds of metres, over or into enemy fortifications. Like its big brother, this Mini Weapon will have to be adjusted for accuracy. But once you've mastered its construction, you'll soon be building larger versions capable of tossing pianos and compact cars over your neighbour's house.

SUPPLIES	TOOLS	AMMO
8 large paper clips	Safety glasses	1+ pencil rubbers
Cardboard	Needle-nose pliers	
Masking or duct tape	Scissors	RANGE
1 D battery	Pen	
String		3–6m

>>>

STEP 1

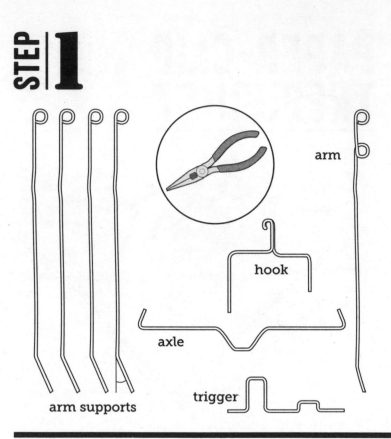

arm

hook

axle

trigger

arm supports

To begin, you will need to bend and cut eight large paper clips. First, straighten out all the large paper clips, then use the illustration above as an overlay as you rebend the straightened clips. To create the four arm supports, use a pair of needle-nose pliers to add one loop to the end of four clips. The opposite end of each arm support should have a slight angle in it.

To create the arm, bend the straightened clip in the same way as the arm supports, but add one additional loop under the end loop.

The hook should be bent to a width that fits around the D battery. Use the reference to bend the axle and trigger into their shapes; these paper clips may need to be cut down in size to match the overlay. Some additional bending and modification will take place as you construct the trebuchet.

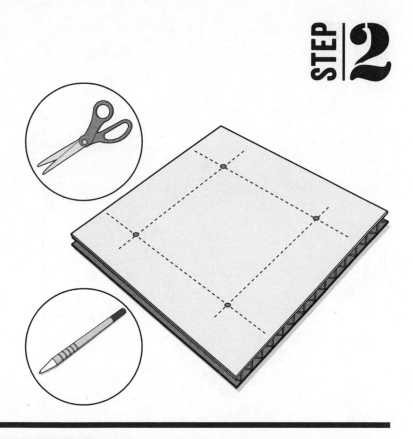

Bring on the base! Cut a piece of corrugated cardboard to be approximately 14cm by 14cm. Corrugated cardboard from a shipping box is ideal because of the material's depth, perfect to burrow in the paper clip supports. If corrugated cardboard is not available, thin cardboard can work as well, but some additional taping will be needed.

Now, with a pen, draw out a box that is approximately 7.5cm wide by 9cm long, more or less centred on the cardboard surface. At the four corners of the box, draw circles to mark your four support holes.

STEP 3

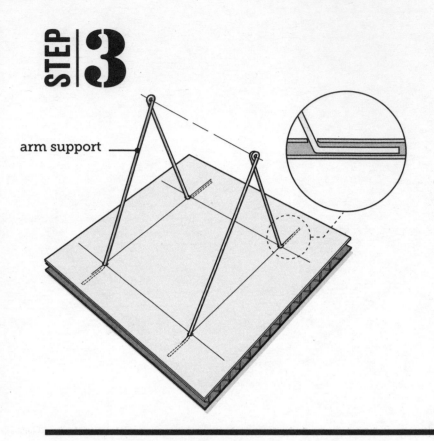

arm support

Now it's time for some support. Push the angled end of each support into the cardboard at the corners you marked on your box, facing out as shown. With the four support bars in place, line up the loop ends so they touch one another in pairs.

If you are using thin cardboard for the base, you will need to pierce the surface and tape the arm supports to the underside of the cardboard. This tape will not only hold the supports in place but also prevent them from scratching the tabletop.

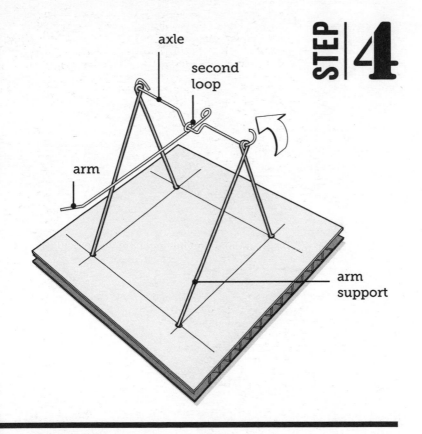

Now slide the axle through the second loop on the launching arm. Once the arm is attached to the axle, slide the axle ends into the arm-support loops.

Once in place, with the axle notch pointing down, bend the ends of the axle arms up to hold everything in place. You may need to use the pliers for this. The axle shouldn't be movable, so if needed, use tape to add additional support to the axle. Your design should resemble a child's swing set. If you feel your frame is still unstable, add two more paper clips for side supports, as seen on the final illustration (page 157).

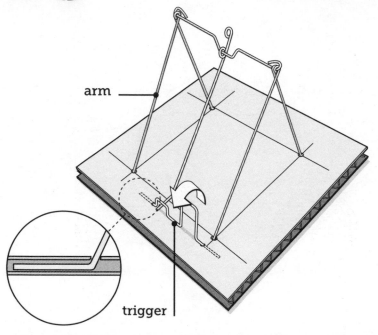

arm

trigger

Now position the arm forwards so that it's resting on the cardboard surface. This will determine the location of your trigger. You will be installing the trigger much like the supports, by running its ends under the cardboard. Poke the ends of the modified clip into the corrugated cardboard so that the small trigger notch aligns with the arm tip, as shown above. The small notch in the bar holds the trebuchet arm, while the large notch is for your finger.

The trigger works when you flip the finger tap down, releasing the arm. Test your mechanism clearance before you install the battery weight.

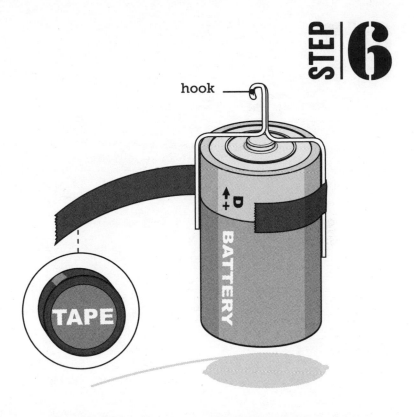

hook

Bend the custom hook around the battery so it fits snugly around the housing. The hook should be located above the centre point of the battery. Once correctly bent, securely tape the battery and hook together.

If a D battery is unavailable, three or four smaller batteries or a roll of coins can be taped together to create the counter-weight instead.

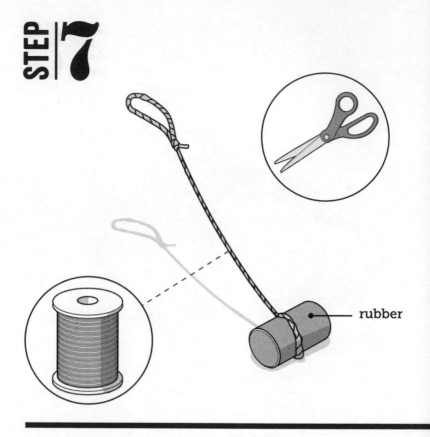

rubber

Now it's time to construct your ammunition. Because these things go flying, it may be worthwhile to make several before launching them.

Start with a 12.5-cm piece of heavy thread or kite string. Tie one end into a loop, then tie the opposite end around a rubber pulled from a pencil. If the knot doesn't look like it's going to hold, add some tape or glue.

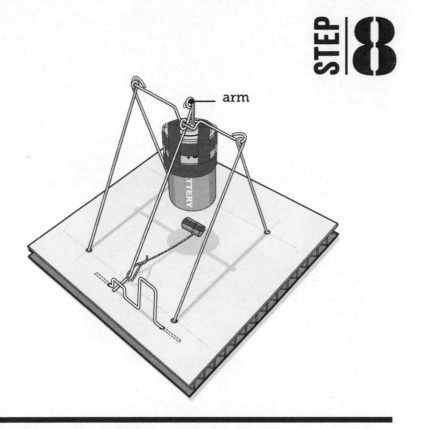

arm

Your Trebuchet is almost complete. Take the counterweight battery and hook it onto the last loop available on the launch arm, as shown. If you let it go, the weight should spring the arm upwards. The battery should not touch the cardboard surface when the arm flings up, so if this happens, shorten the battery hook.

Next, place your ammunition loop over the opposite end of the launch arm. Then place the string and rubber underneath the framework so that they don't interfere with the trigger mechanism.

Now set the trigger so that it holds the launch arm down. When you're set to fire the trebuchet, put on your safety glasses, pull back the finger tab, and watch with amazement. Adjust as necessary for the desired results.

5

COMBUSTION SHOOTERS

AIRSOFT PEN POPPER

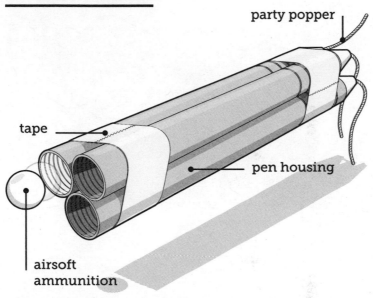

party popper

tape

pen housing

airsoft
ammunition

It's party time! This multi-shooter packs a one-two-three punch against any target. With impressive firing velocity and a pocket-sized frame, it's the perfect companion for a well-equipped marksman.

SUPPLIES

3 party poppers
3 pens
Transparent or
    masking tape

TOOLS

Safety glasses
Scissors

AMMO

3+ airsoft BBs,
    .24 calibre (6mm)

RANGE
6–12m

STEP | 1

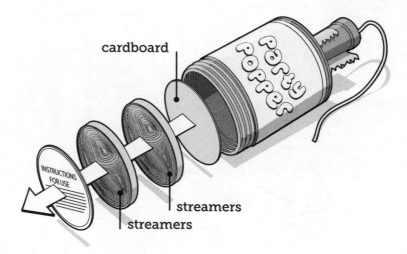

cardboard

INSTRUCTIONS
FOR USE

party
POPPer

streamers

streamers

To start, you'll need party poppers that have a pull-string trigger. These loud products are designed to fill a room with colourful streamers. Because they are not considered fire-works, you can buy them at most major shops that carry party supplies. Use your finger or the end of a writing utensil to remove the streamers and cardboard. This will make it easier to locate the explosive charge in the next step.

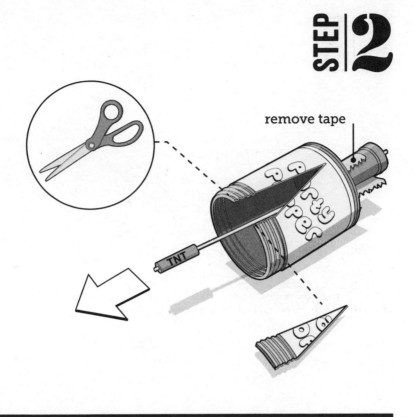

remove tape

Now it's time to pull out the popper's explosive innards. Remember to put on your safety glasses. Then, remove the tape or decorative foil around the neck.

Using scissors, cut a section out of the side of the party popper. This will provide room for your fingers to grab the explosive charge. Once you have it, slowly slide it out with the string still attached. If it feels like it's not coming out, **don't yank it** – this might detonate the explosive charge. Once the charge is removed, you can discard the popper housing.

AIRSOFT PEN POPPER

STEP 3

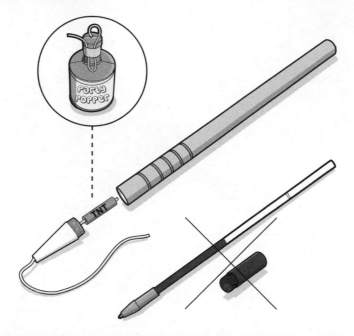

Your pen should be a ballpoint or roller-ball pen with an unscrewable metal tip. These are generally inexpensive, and you are likely to have a few lying around.

Disassemble the pen and remove its ink cartridge, metal tip, and plastic end. Discard the ink cartridge and plastic end.

Now take your party-popper charge and push the string through the metal pen tip. Gently pull it all the way through until the charge is nestled into the metal cone. Once it's in place, screw the tip back into the pen.

Next, tape the metal tip onto the pen as an extra precaution. Depending on the manufacturer and materials, there is always the chance for the unexpected to occur.

Load your .24 calibre (6 mm) airsoft ammo into the muzzle end of your barrel. These BBs are very inexpensive and usually fit perfectly into pen housings. To fire the popper, simply aim and pull the popper string.

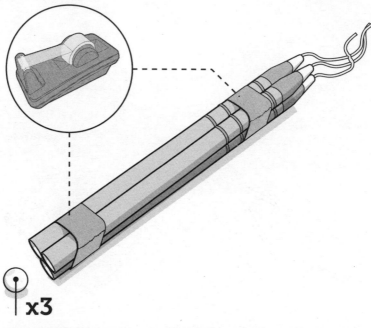

x3

If you want to fire multiple shots in a short time, tape three pen housings together, each preloaded with an explosive charge. Pull the strings individually to give yourself multiple shot opportunities.

You can also substitute ammunition and use a good old-fashioned spitball or the original streamers. Just use one of the ink cartridges to ram the ammunition down into the pen barrel prior to firing. These are safer alternatives than BBs, but you will not achieve the same firing distance.

Never aim your Airsoft Pen Popper at a human or animal! A BB ricochet is probable, so always wear safety glasses when firing. And *never look down the barrel*, even with safety glasses on.

MATCH ROCKETS

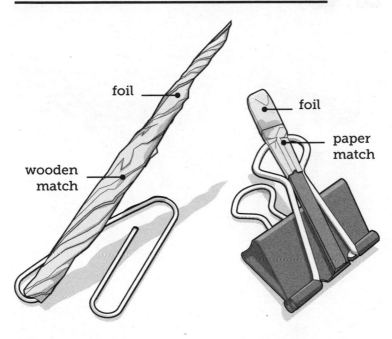

foil

foil

paper
match

wooden
match

Match Rockets are a very inexpensive way to learn about basic rocketry and can be made with paper matches or wooden matches. They are unpredictable and can fly in any direction, making it interesting to see where they might land, but *eye protection and a safe firing range are musts* when experimenting with these mini jets.

SUPPLIES

Aluminium foil
1 needle or pin
1 medium foldback
   clip (32 mm)
1 toothpick
1 large paper clip

TOOLS

Safety glasses
Penknife

AMMO

1+ paper matches
4+ wooden matches

RANGE

6–12m

STEP | 1

PAPER MATCH ROCKET

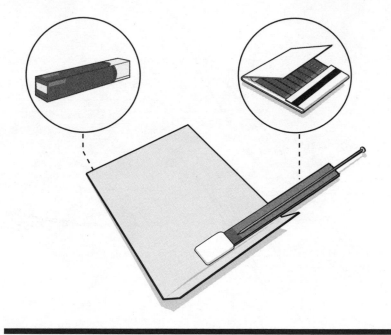

Start by building a Paper Match Rocket. Remove a paper match from a matchbook. Place it onto a small piece of aluminium foil, no more than 2.5cm by 2.5cm. Then place a needle or pin onto the paper handle, as shown. This needle will form your exhaust port in the next step.

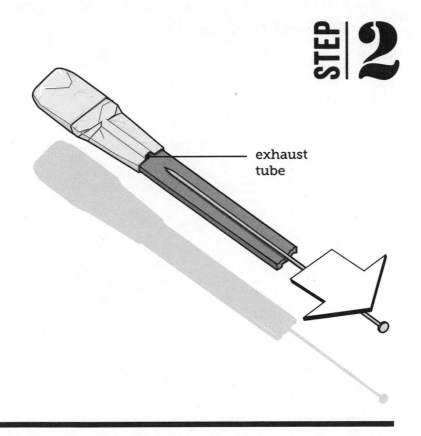

exhaust
tube

Roll the aluminium foil over the top half of the match. Make sure you tightly form the foil over the phosphorus head of the match and around the pin or needle protruding from it.

Once the match is wrapped, slowly slide the needle out of the aluminium wrapping without reshaping the foil. The pin has created an air channel that goes directly to the match head. This will be the rocket's exhaust port. Handle the rocket with care before launching to avoid crushing this channel. A crushed exhaust port will cause a blowout or misfire.

STEP | 3

Put on your safety glasses. Place your Paper Match Rocket on a foldback clip launcher, head up, pointed away from you. It's a good idea to protect the surface from which you're launching your rocket. A Paper Match Rocket is capable of burning surfaces and igniting flammable material, so careful outdoor use is a must.

Now hold a lit match beneath the rocket's head. Wait a few seconds for the flame's heat to penetrate the aluminium foil and ignite the paper match. Once lit, the burning head will create pressure and shoot gases out of the exhaust port of your mini jet. This force will propel your rocket into space.

If your rocket lights up but doesn't fly, it's because the gases couldn't make it down the exhaust port. Rebuild the rocket and try again.

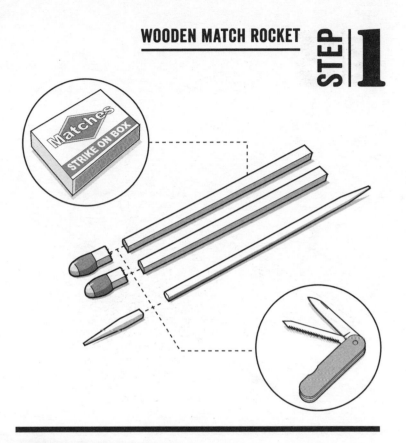

I personally find Paper Match Rockets the easiest type of match rocket to fire. However, I've also found that Wooden Match Rockets fly a greater distance, which is why I've included designs for both types. Note: Wooden matches vary by manufacturer, as do their rocketry results.

Now it's time to build a Wooden Match Rocket. Take two wooden matches and cut off the phosphorous-coated head with a penknife. Keep the heads and discard the sticks.

Next, take a round wooden toothpick and remove one of the points from the end with a penknife. Discard the point and save the toothpick.

Cut a small square of aluminium foil with sides that are approximately the same length as a wooden match. You must have enough material to roll up the match heads several times. If the walls of your rocket are too thin, you will have a blowout problem and a fire on the launch pad. But on the flip side, if the walls are too thick, the added weight will decrease the distance your rocket travels.

Along one edge of the foil, make a straight fold. This crease will help you line up the materials. Place the two match heads facing each other on the inside of the fold, an approximately equal distance from the edges of the foil. Then place the cut, blunt end of the round toothpick behind one of the match heads, as shown.

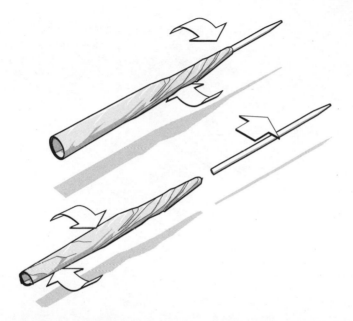

Without spilling the match heads, tightly roll the foil around them and the toothpick. Then roll the front of the aluminium rocket head to form a crude missile tip. Finally, slowly pull out the wooden toothpick. The toothpick will have created a cylindrical hole leading up to the match heads. Do not disturb or squeeze this end or the exhaust port.

Your Match Rocket is now ready for the launch pad!

STEP 4

Make a launch pad for your Wooden Match Rocket by partially unbending a large paper clip to form the base, then pivoting one of the ends upwards to form a guide for your rocket. Once your launch platform is bent into shape, slide the bottom of your rocket over the end of the paper clip launcher.

Put on your safety glasses. Hold a burning match under the covered match heads and wait for ignition. If the match heads burn through the foil wall, it means either that your rocket needs to be wrapped a few more times or that your exhaust port was blocked.

Remember, you are shooting a flaming match, so use these rockets outdoors and remove all flammable materials from the launch zone. A match rocket is capable of burning any surface it lands on.

MINI SPUD-AND-SPIT

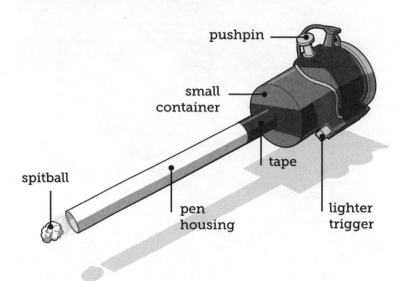

pushpin

small container

spitball

tape

pen housing

lighter trigger

This Mini Spud-and-Spit gun is a perfect way of launching spitballs. Similar to a firearm or potato gun, it works by pushing the projectile out of the barrel using expanding gas.

SUPPLIES

1 barbecue lighter
2 pushpins
1 small container
   (with cap)
1 pen
Electrical tape
Hairspray

TOOLS

Safety glasses
Screwdriver
Wire cutter
Craft knife

AMMO

Spitballs

RANGE
6–12m

STEP 1

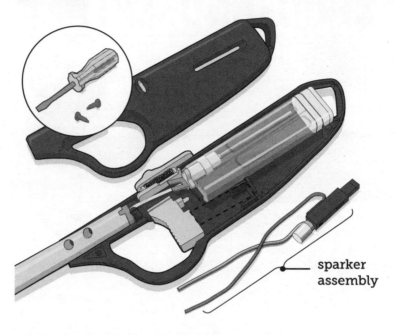

sparker assembly

Focus first on the ignition source. Use a screwdriver to open up your barbecue lighter. Once you've opened it, locate the sparker assembly behind the trigger. Remove the unit and wires, keeping them intact, but be careful not to shock your-self by pushing the button. (You won't need the rest of the lighter, so discard the other components, including the fluid.)

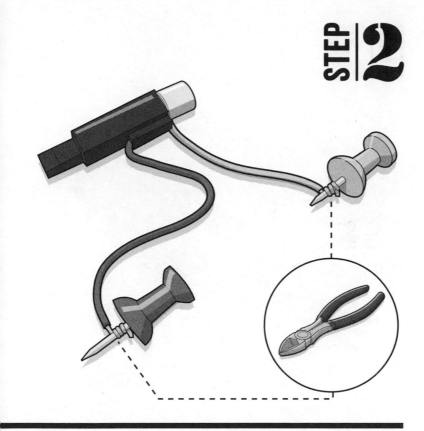

Using a wire cutter, trim the plastic insulation from the last couple of centimetres of both wires, taking care to avoid cutting the wires themselves.

Tightly wrap each exposed wire end around the metal point of a pushpin. These pushpins will act as your electrodes in the Mini Spud-and-Spit's combustion chamber.

STEP 3

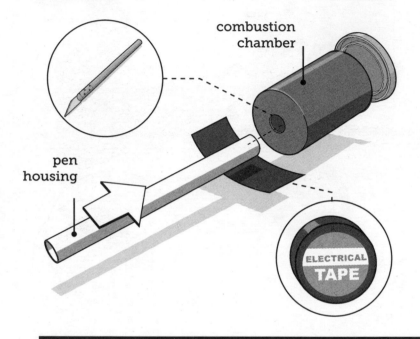

combustion chamber

pen housing

ELECTRICAL TAPE

Your airtight combustion chamber must have a cap that can be easily removed and closed during operation. In this design, you will be using an old film roll container for the chamber.

Empty a pen housing of all its contents. Then, with a craft knife, carefully cut a hole in the bottom of your combustion chamber; the hole should have a diameter exactly the same size as a pen-housing barrel.

Once you have carved out a hole, slide the barrel into the combustion chamber and tape it into place. The barrel and chamber should be airtight, so don't be stingy with the tape.

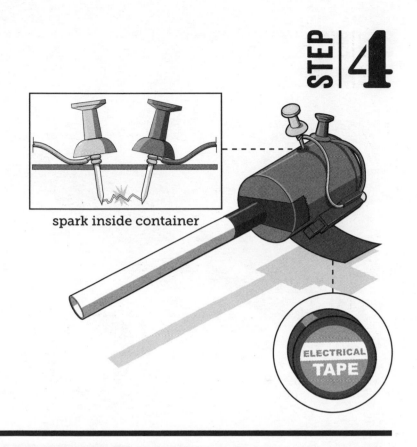

spark inside container

Now to attach your ignition system. Stick the two pushpins into the combustion chamber near the rear of the chamber roughly half a centimetre apart from one another. Then, using electrical tape, attach the trigger from the barbecue lighter to the side of the film roll container. Wrap vigorously with electrical tape before testing.

Once the trigger is taped on, test your ignition system. Push the small switch on the trigger and make sure the push-pins are sparking inside the chamber.

If your ignition system is not sparking, the metal ends of the pushpins may not be close enough or the electricity may be arcing outside of the canister, so rework the wires until you get it right.

Now for the easy part, create a spitball in your mouth. Push the wet ball into the muzzle end of the Mini Weapon's barrel. Use the pen's ink cartridge to help push the spitball to the rear of the barrel but not into the combustion chamber.

Now add the aerosol hairspray (which contains alcohol, propane or butane) to the combustion chamber. (Only a small burst of hairspray is needed for this micro-launcher.) Then quickly cap the chamber and aim it carefully. Trigger the ignition switch and watch the spitball fly.

Just like with every spitball, your results can also vary using the Mini Spud-and-Spit. Variables include container size, barrel length, spitball size, hairspray amount and the specific mixture of aerosol used in the hairspray.

PING-PONG ZOOKA

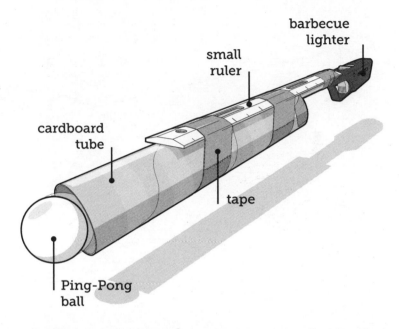

barbecue lighter

small ruler

cardboard tube

tape

Ping-Pong ball

The Ping-Pong Zooka is one of the only launchers you're likely to see that sends flames flying out of its cardboard muzzle. The zooka is a low-range combustion shooter that uses non-threatening Ping-Pong ammunition. With its quick build time, you'll soon be launching balls of fury!

SUPPLIES

1 cardboard tube
Duct tape
1 barbecue lighter
1 small ruler
Hairspray

TOOLS

Safety glasses
Craft knife

AMMO

1+ Ping-Pong balls

RANGE

6m

STEP 1

Paper towel cardboard tubes vary in size, so before you begin, check the diameter of your tube against the circumference of the Ping-Pong ball. It should be a snug fit.

Using duct tape, cover one end of the paper towel tube. Now, with a craft knife, create a small incision in the duct tape cover. The diameter of this hole should be the same size as the nozzle on the barbecue lighter you'll be using.

barbecue
lighter

Install the zooka's ignition source by inserting the lighter nozzle through the duct tape incision at the end of the cardboard tube. The nozzle should extend 2.5cm to 5cm into the cardboard tube.

Use duct tape to seal any opening remaining around the tape incision. This seal will prevent the loss of combustion, so use as much tape as you need to ensure a tight seal.

STEP 3

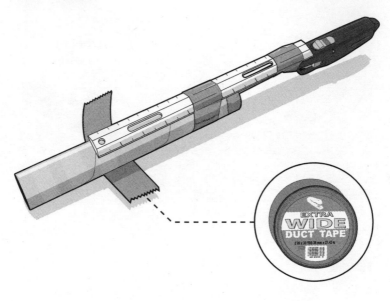

To add some much needed support to your Ping-Pong Zooka, duct tape a plastic or wooden ruler on top of the assembly. It should bridge the tube and lighter assemblies. This will allow you to keep one of your hands free while loading and firing.

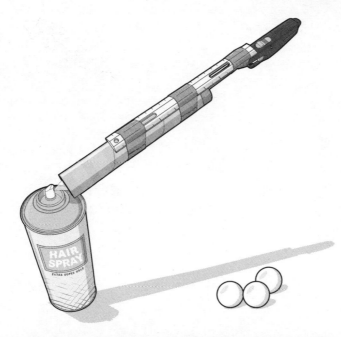

Hold your Ping-Pong Zooka so that the muzzle end of the barrel is lower than the combustion chamber. Shoot a small amount of a slightly flammable aerosol hairspray or body spray (it should contain alcohol, propane or butane) into the cardboard tube. The flammable vapour will make it to the rear of the combustion chamber, right where you need it.

Immediately after spraying the aerosol into the cardboard barrel, insert the Ping-Pong ball. Safely aim your launcher and press the trigger. It is a good idea to add only a small amount of hairspray the first time and then gradually increase it until you find a safe and appropriate amount to launch your Ping-Pong ball.

6

MINI BOMBS AND CLAYMORE MINE

MATCHBOX BOMB

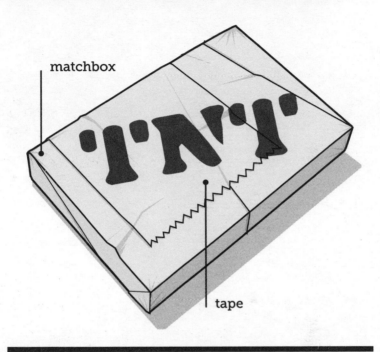

matchbox

tape

This matchbox marvel will certainly have your neighbours jumping for cover. Designed to be thrown, the matchbox bomb is a perfect ear-piercing weapon. The design makes it ideal for any soldier to experiment with, using different-sized boxes to meet his or her mission's specific goals.

SUPPLIES

1 box of matches
Masking or
    duct tape

TOOLS

Safety glasses
Earplugs
Scissors

AMMO

Matches

RANGE

1.5m

STEP | 1

For this mini bomb, you will need a box (any size) of wooden stick matches with a striking surface.

First, remove the cover from the matchbox. Use scissors or a craft knife to slice off the striking surface on the side of the box. Save both the striking surface and the remaining box for the next steps.

striking surface

Once the striking surface has been removed, slide it in front of the match heads inside the box. Slide the remaining box cover over the box of matches to conceal the contents and keep the matches from falling out.

STEP |3

TAPE

Tape the matchbox securely, using several layers of tape if necessary, to confine its explosive contents. Once wrapped, throw the box with all your might against a hard surface outdoors. The phosphorus match heads will ignite when they rub the striking surface. The gases released from the combusting matches will need to escape, causing a small-scale explosion.

As always, remember: *safety first!* Keep the Matchbook Bomb away from flammable materials and never use it indoors. The matchbox can be unstable, so handle it with care before detonation. This Matchbox Bomb is also capable of producing loud noises, so earplugs and eye protection are recommended. Use at your own risk.

PENNY BOMB

coin —————————— 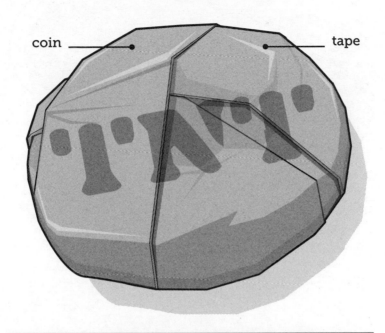 ———————————— tape

Penny Bombs get their explosive power from paper caps. Caps for toy guns are available to buy in bulk in large rolls, which will have you blasting every penny you have. Once you learn to build these sound grenades, you'll be covering your ears in no time.

SUPPLIES

100 paper caps
Transparent or
    masking tape

TOOLS

Safety glasses
Earplugs

AMMO

1 penny

RANGE

6m

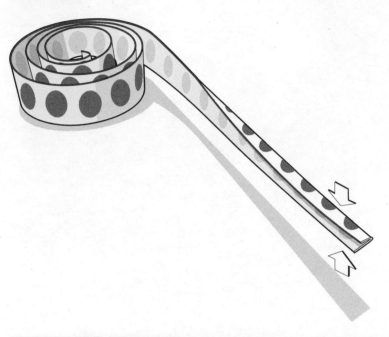

Unroll your caps on a smooth surface. Then fold the paper down the middle to reduce the width by half. The number of caps you use is your decision; however, 100 caps is more than adequate for a single Penny Bomb.

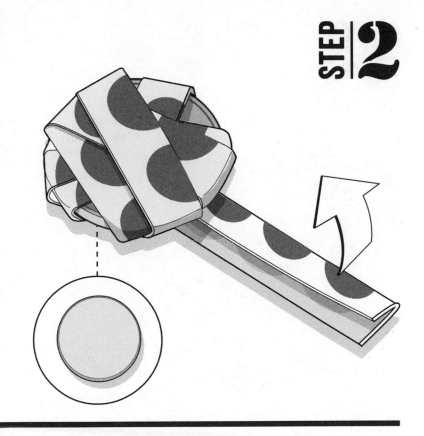

Take the folded paper caps and tightly wrap them around a penny several times, overlapping each previous layer until you have dramatically increased the size of the coin. The coin will add much needed weight to the Penny Bomb when you throw it.

STEP 3

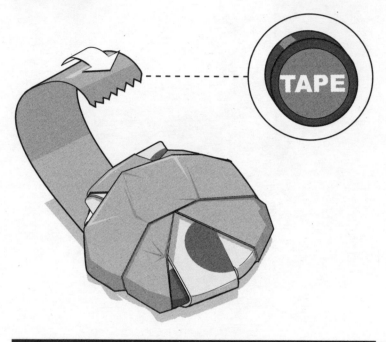

TAPE

Once the folded caps are wrapped around the coin, tape them in place. In this case, the less tape you use the better.

Take your mini bomb outside and throw it against the pavement. It is capable of producing loud noises, so ear and eye protection are recommended. Always keep safety in mind, and never throw a Penny Bomb at anyone.

WATER BOMB

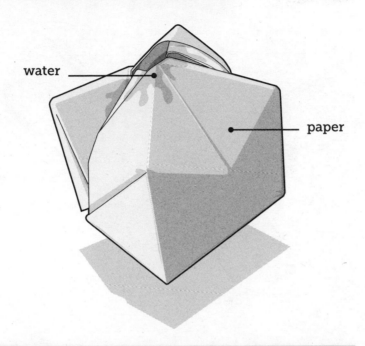

water

paper

The Water Bomb is constructed using only one sheet of paper and your origami skills to form a small container capable of holding water. Once filled, time is of the essence. Throw your water grenade at the unsuspecting target, and on impact it will break apart, drenching your victim.

SUPPLIES

1 sheet of paper

TOOLS

Scissors

AMMO

Water

RANGE

6m

STEP 1

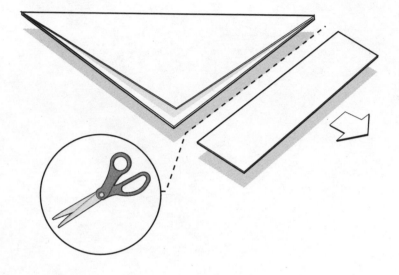

Take a standard-sized piece of paper and fold it diagonally as shown. Then use scissors to trim off the extra rectangle. Discard the trimmed piece and unfold the triangle to find a perfect square of paper.

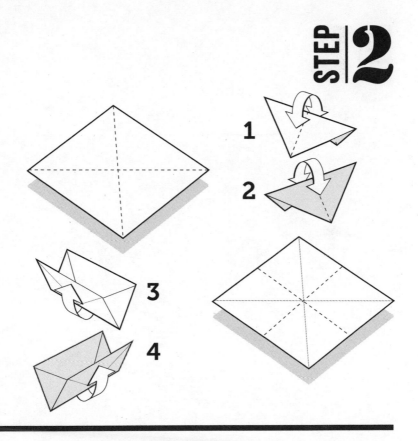

Now for some creative folding. Fold the paper along the other diagonal and then in half both ways until you have what appears to be a star pattern. Use the illustration above for reference. This may take a few tries due to the confusing nature of the creases.

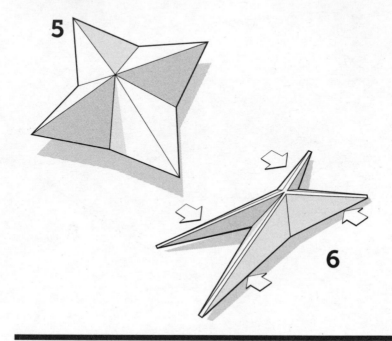

5

6

Pull the centre point forward while pushing in at the centre of the four edges to form a star. Once this is completed, run your fingers along the fold lines to crease the edges. This will help the paper keep its form during construction.

Finally, carefully push in the two adjacent sides to form a quadruple-walled triangle.

MINI BOMBS AND CLAYMORE MINE

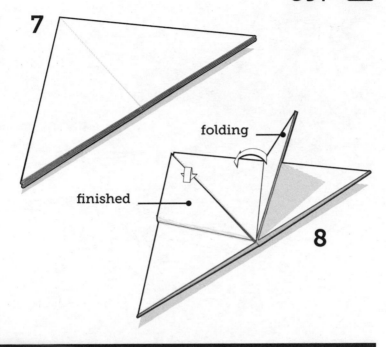

7

folding

finished

8

Next, take the thick paper triangle and lay it flat with the bottom edge facing you.

Fold the bottom right corner towards the centre to form a smaller triangle. The corner should reach up to the top point. Repeat this step with the bottom left corner. When finished you will have created a diamond shape on this side. Crease the edges with your finger.

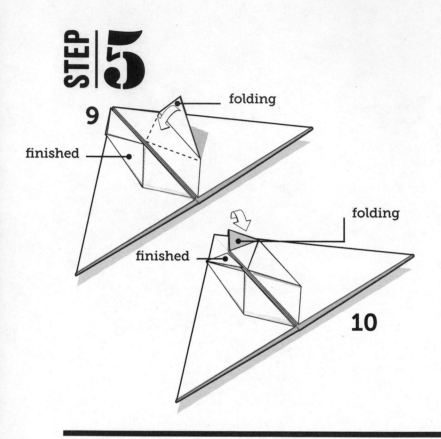

Take the left and right points of your diamond and fold them inwards, to the centreline, creating two smaller triangles. See the illustration for reference.

Next, fold down the top of these smaller triangles so they are flush with the other two triangles, as shown.

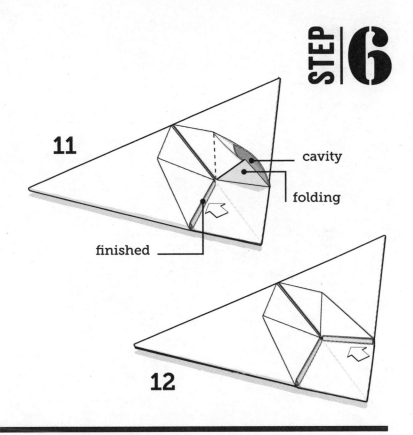

11

cavity

folding

finished

12

Rotate the triangle so that the point faces you.

Fold one of the smallest of the triangles into the cavity right below it (which was created when you folded in the side of the diamond earlier). It will take some work to get it nestled in place. Repeat this step for the adjacent side.

This completes the folding on this side. Now you will have to flip over the paper triangle and repeat steps 4, 5, and 6.

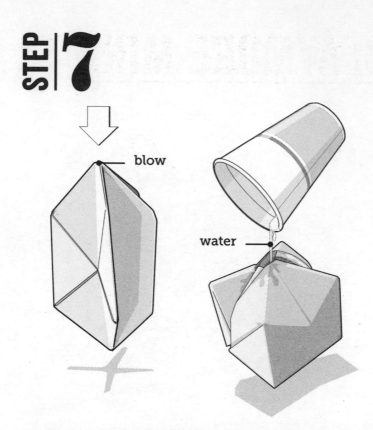

The Water Bomb is now finished – it's time to add air. Locate the end with the hole in it and blow into it as hard as you can to inflate the paper box. You may need to use your hands to gently help the paper balloon open and take shape.

When you know your target's arrival is near, fill the paper box with water and lie in wait. Once the target is in sight, launch your Water Bomb. It is important to keep in mind that the Water Bomb won't last long once it's filled with water, so you must act quickly. The slow grenadier gets wet.

CLAYMORE MINE

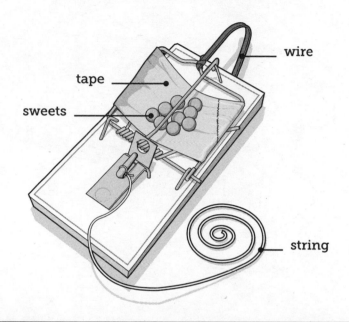

wire

tape

sweets

string

The Claymore Mine is a self-setting miniature land mine that is capable of firing sweet shrapnel – perfect for ambushing any biscuit-stealing intruders. This basic design can be used for creating a perimeter matrix or scaring someone. It also makes an awesome tool during a game of cops and robbers.

SUPPLIES

Speaker wire
1 mousetrap
Tape (any kind)
String

TOOLS

Safety glasses
Wire cutter
Stapler

AMMO

Sweets

RANGE
6m

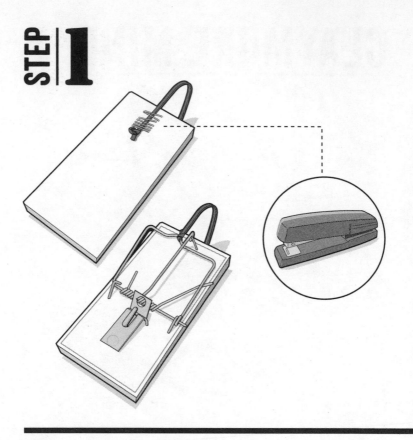

Cut approximately 15cm of speaker wire to harness your spring mechanism. Tie one end of the speaker wire to the mousetrap bar. Then, using staples or a screw, fasten the other end of the speaker cord to the bottom of the mousetrap. Adjust the length of the cord so that, once set, the swinging mouse-trap bar only rotates a half or a quarter of the rotation to its normal, closed position. Where this bar stops will determine the direction your shrapnel flies.

STEP 2

TAPE

Holding the mousetrap face up, use tape to create a concave pouch on top of the mousetrap bar. This tape will act as the launching platform for your sugary shrapnel.

STEP | 3

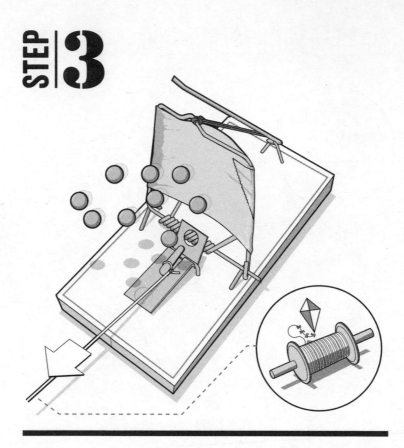

Strong string or high-test fishing line is perfect for the trip line. Tie one end of the line to the cheese trigger on the mousetrap. Now find a great location close to the ground and tape the mousetrap into place. Leaving no slack, tie the other end of the line to something permanently stationary. Set your trap and carefully place your small sweets onto the launch pad – then wait.

If using the Claymore Mine on the lawn or outside, add small spikes to your device by drilling large screws through the mousetrap's wooden frame and into the ground.

Always wear your safety glasses when playing with this Mini Weapon. The shrapnel will fly in every direction, so use at your own risk.

ALTERNATE CONSTRUCTION

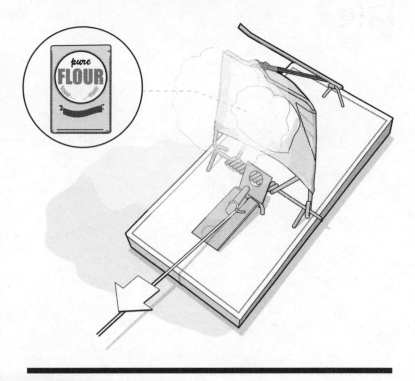

Looking for a realistic smoke explosion? Add baking flour to the shrapnel pouch. Once the line is hit and the shrapnel is released, the flour will go flying, making a dusty cloud. This is a great addition to your indoor mini arsenal.

7

CONCEALING BOOK AND TARGETS

CONCEALING BOOK

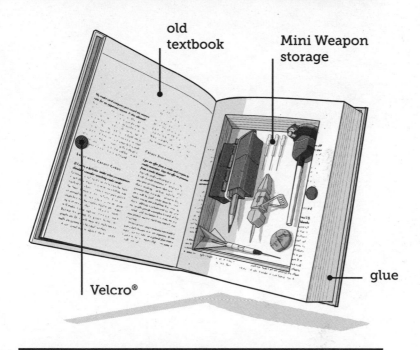

old textbook

Mini Weapon storage

Velcro®

glue

This hollowed-out book serves as a secret safe for stashing all your Mini Weapons of Mass Destruction. It's the perfect tool for unannounced room raids, and it can also be used to hide cash to finance your mini rebellion.

SUPPLIES

1 old textbook
1 plastic freezer bag
White glue
1 paper or plastic cup
Water
Velcro

TOOLS

Paintbrush
Ruler
Craft knife
Pencil or pen
Hot glue gun
   (optional)

>>>

STEP 1

Place a plastic freezer bag as a marker somewhere in the last few pages of the textbook you plan to use for your Concealing Book. This will help control the running adhesive and protect your work surface.

Pour some white glue into a paper cup and mix in water – about two parts water to one part glue. Brush the mixture onto the sides of the textbook pages.

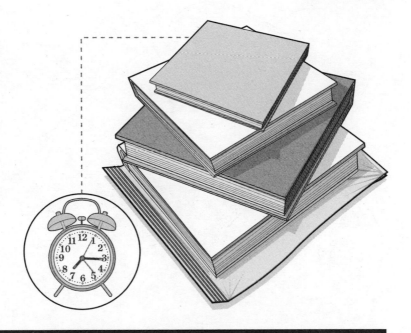

Once you've finished coating the sides thoroughly, let the glue dry. The damp pages will have a tendency to wrinkle while drying. To prevent this, stack something heavy (more text-books will do nicely) on top of the drying book.

Once the adhesive is dry, go back and add a second coat. Allow it to dry, too.

STEP 3

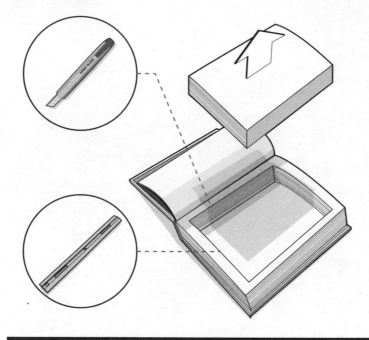

Now that your book has dried, it's time to cut out the centre compartment. Use a ruler to mark out the compartment size you would like. Once you have your lines, use a sharp craft knife to gradually cut out the layers of pages. Having the sides of the book glued will make this step easier. Discard the page sections you cut out.

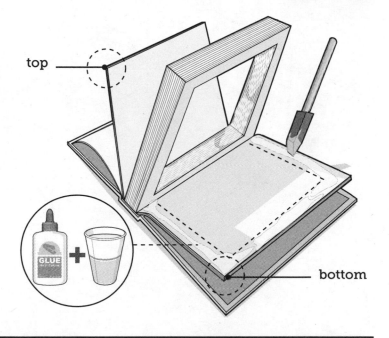

top

bottom

Now it's time to add the compartment bottom. You can either hot glue the compartment to the back cover of the book or use white glue to fuse together the last few pages of the book; a couple of pages stuck together will form a solid bottom.

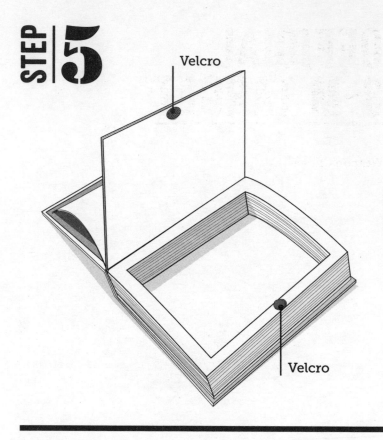

Velcro

Velcro

For extra security, add small opposing pieces of Velcro with adhesive backing to your compartment cover as illustrated. This will help keep it closed when picked up. You don't want to lose your precious cargo or expose your hiding spot.

OFFICIAL
3-M TARGET

Weapon Choice _____

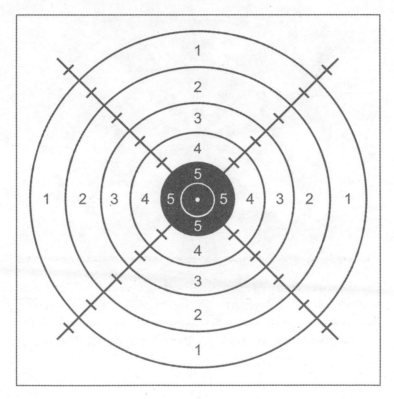

Competitor _____ Date _____

Competitor Signature _____

Use a photocopier to make multiples and enlarge

DARTBOARD TARGET

Weapon Choice _____

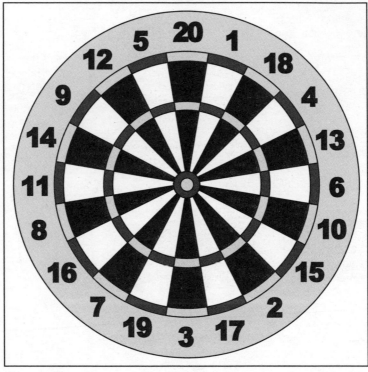

	20	19	18	17	16	15	Bull
P1	○○○	○○○	○○○	○○○	○○○	○○○	○○○
P2	○○○	○○○	○○○	○○○	○○○	○○○	○○○
P3	○○○	○○○	○○○	○○○	○○○	○○○	○○○

Competitor _____ Date _____

Competitor Signature _____

Use a photocopier to make multiples and enlarge

ZOMBIE TARGET

Use a photocopier to make multiples and enlarge

For more information and free
downloadable targets, please visit:

MINIWEAPONSBOOK.COM

*Don't forget to join the
Mini Weapons Army on Facebook:*

Mini Weapons of Mass Destruction:
Homemade Weapons Page